Centre for
Faith and Spirituality
Loughborough University

Making Connections

Exploring Methodist Deacons' Perspectives
on Contemporary Diaconal Ministry

— ANDREW ORTON & TODD STOCKDALE —

Durham
University
School of Applied Social Sciences

WESLEY
STUDY CENTRE
DURHAM
For All God's People to Serve the Present Age

The **Methodist** Church

D0301251

Sacristy
Press

Sacristy Press
PO Box 612, Durham, DH1 9HT

www.sacristy.co.uk

First published in 2014 by Sacristy Press, Durham

British Library Cataloguing-in-Publication Data
A catalogue record for the book is available from the British Library

Paperback ISBN 978–1–908381–19–4
Hardback ISBN 978–1–908381–94–1

FOREWORD

This book has provided a vital and valuable opportunity for the voices of deacons to be heard, and to recognise the creative, pioneering and diverse ministries being exercised by deacons across the Methodist Church in Britain. The Ministries Committee of the Methodist Church welcomes this opportunity for a full and open discussion with voices from the wider Church, to celebrate the gifts of diaconal ministry and to recognise and address its challenges.

This book provides a helpful and fascinating snapshot of diaconal practices and perceptions. There is inevitably a strong degree of variation among the observations and perceptions expressed in the book, which are not necessarily representative of the views of the Ministries Committee and the Methodist Church in Britain. However, it is immensely valuable to have gathered together in one place the thoughts and experiences of deacons from every area group across the Connexion.[1]

The Methodist Church continues its commitment to the nurturing of scholarship, research and innovation, and is pleased to have been able to support this particular piece of work through Connexional funding. Through the Discipleship and Ministries Learning Network, the Connexion will continue to support research projects like this which allow us to better understand, resource and develop the life of the Church.

The research contained within this book will, we are certain, be the subject of careful reflection across the Connexion, and a continuing dialogue with the governance bodies of the Methodist Church. This work has already been fed back to the Methodist Diaconal Order, where it has been gratefully acknowledged. We, the Ministries Committee, are grateful to all those who have contributed to this book for the opportunity to engage in a conversation and to further the Church's understanding of the gifts and challenges of diaconal ministry in the Methodist Church.

Ministries Committee
The Methodist Church in Britain
January 2013

NOTES

1. "Connexion" is a Methodist term that refers to the larger connected community of the national Methodist Church, including its informal networks and formal organisational structures.

ACKNOWLEDGEMENTS

The authors would like to express their thanks to all those who have contributed to the two year project that led to this publication. Particular thanks are expressed to:

- The Methodist Church in Britain, for funding the project.
- The Revd Dr Roger Walton, in his former role as Director of the Wesley Study Centre, for seeing the potential in the project at the start and supporting the initial application to get it established.
- The Revd Dr Calvin Samuel, as the current Director of the Wesley Study Centre, and the wider Wesley Study Centre staff and students, for continuing to host the project, and for making the authors part of their immensely-supportive team.
- Loraine Richardson, Penny Bissell and John Major, for organising the "Making Connections: Exploring Contemporary Diaconal Ministry" conference with the authors, and all the speakers and attendees at this conference, for contributing to stimulating discussions when the findings were presented to the wider Church.
- The School of Applied Social Sciences at Durham University, for enabling Dr Andrew Orton's continued contribution as part of his new academic role as a Lecturer in Community and Youth Work within the university.
- Dr Mark Powell, for contributing to the data analysis process.
- Deacon Vincent Purcell, for providing support to the project at a key time, and for reflecting ecumenically with us on the findings and their implications for practice.
- The Reference Group, consisting of Prof. Jeff Astley, Deacon Eunice Attwood, The Revd Dr Brian Beck, Deacon Sue Culver, Canon Dr Paula Gooder, The Revd Ken Howcroft, Mrs Susan Howdle, and The Revd Dr Mark Wakelin, who provided comments which helped clarify early drafts of this publication.
- All those who have contributed for their insights and time.
- And last, but definitely not least, the Methodist Diaconal Order, without whom the research would not have been possible, and whose

generous sharing of their ministry and expertise forms the heart of this work.

The authors have always seen this research (and the production of this publication in particular) as only one stage in a broader ongoing process of dialogue between deacons and those with whom they work, that is necessarily wider than this particular study. As with any research, there is always more that could be done, and other approaches which would add further important perspectives to those gathered and reported here. However, it is our hope that what is offered in this publication provides a helpful contribution to these wider discussions. We particularly hope that this contribution will be engaged with constructively and critically by deacons and others, in ways that both further the understanding of this ministry and support the development of the wider Church.

Andrew Orton and Todd Stockdale

CONTENTS

FIGURES

1.   INTRODUCTION

1.1.   WHY DOES DIACONAL MINISTRY MATTER IN THE CONTEMPORARY GLOBAL CONTEXT?[1]

Across the world, those seeking to live out lives of Christian faith are facing considerable challenges as they endeavour to apply their faith in rapidly changing and increasingly diverse societies.[2] Many religious groups continue to make substantial contributions within local communities, not least through their social welfare and international development activities.[3] However, the place of religion within society and the contribution of action motivated by faith both continue to receive increasingly critical scrutiny.[4] Reasons for this scrutiny include the development of contested processes of secularisation in many nations, which have challenged the place of religious groups and perspectives in the public arena. This scrutiny has intensified thanks to the ways in which some forms of religion have often become implicated in social division, abuses of power, conflict and violence in local communities across the globe.[5] In this context, churches have engaged in significant debates about how they understand their mission in the wider world,[6] and how they can continue to build improved connections between the Christian faith, churches, and wider communities as part of this mission.[7]

As churches have sought to respond to these contemporary challenges, there has been a remarkable resurgence of interest in renewed forms of diaconal ministry across many Christian denominations around the world.[8] This resurgence is no coincidence as, historically across these contexts, the diaconate has combined significant roles in supporting both the Church and the wider community (especially through service to those considered poor and marginalised). However, since the early Church, this role has also been controversial,[9] not least in terms of *how* it contributes to wider society and the Church, and its implications for wider understandings of social welfare, ministry and mission within these settings. As this book will discuss, the diaconate embodies many of the key theological, missional and ethical challenges facing the Church's engagement with wider society in the current context. This has led various leading publications to comment on how the diaconate may have been created "for such a time as this",[10] whilst also being amongst the "most problematic and most promising"[11] ministries of the Church.

Different Christian denominations across a wide theological spectrum have recognised roles for deacons within their collective life and work. An ecumenical vision of the diaconate is represented in the World Council of Church's landmark "Baptism, Eucharist and Ministry" paper in 1982, which remains relevant today:

> Deacons represent to the Church its calling as servant in the world. By struggling in Christ's name with the myriad needs of societies and persons, deacons exemplify the interdependence of worship and service in the Church's life. They exercise responsibility in the worship of the congregation: for example by reading the scriptures, preaching and leading the people in prayer. They help in the teaching of the congregation. They exercise a ministry of love within the community. They fulfil certain administrative tasks and may be elected to responsibilities for governance.[12]

Despite this collective vision, this paper also recognised in its accompanying commentary that considerable uncertainties existed at the time "about the need, the rationale, the status and the functions of deacons"[13]. Nevertheless, it also noted "a strong tendency in many churches to restore the diaconate as an ordained ministry with its own dignity".[14]

These trends have continued for over thirty years to the present day, with the precise combination of roles undertaken by the diaconate continuing to vary considerably between denominations and contexts. Different denominations have incorporated varying liturgical, organisational leadership, and social service functions within their own understandings.[15] The particular form taken in any particular context has been influenced by the historical and Biblical roots which any particular contemporary manifestation of the diaconate draws upon. For example, some roots of the contemporary resurgence of interest in the diaconate lie in the various renewed forms of diaconal movements that emerged during the Industrial Revolution.[16] These provided opportunities for women in particular to take on prominent roles within Christian social engagement and Church service as deaconesses.[17] These diaconal movements made significant contributions towards the wider growth of welfare services as welfare states developed, with many becoming broader charitable organisations and movements over time.[18] The degree of connection with their founding churches often also changed in this process.[19] In some cases, these renewed diaconal movements drew upon earlier examples of religious orders in organising their work of religiously-inspired charitable service. This included developing models of living as gathered religious communities serving in a particular location, and models which involved dispersed religious orders co-ordinating their work across a wide area.

Other prominent roots of the resurgence of interest in the diaconate lie in the historic understanding and practice of many traditional denominations of seeing the diaconate as a step on the way to becoming a priest.[20] However, drawing on the wider history of this role, some such denominations have also been rediscovering potential roles for "distinctive" deacons who remain in this role permanently.[21] Gender has continued to play a role within these debates, with some denominations historically treating male deacons and female deacons/deaconesses differently.[22] Different denominations have also taken different positions on the related issue of whether the roles of deacons and/or deaconesses are considered as lay or consecrated/ordained roles. The World Council of Churches put the questions relating to these positions as follows:

> In what sense can the diaconate be considered part of the ordained ministry? What is it that distinguishes it from other ministries in the Church (catechists, musicians, etc.)? Why should deacons be ordained while these other ministries do not receive ordination? If they are ordained, do they receive ordination in the full sense of the word or is their ordination only the first step towards ordination as presbyters?[23]

In these ways, diaconal ministry has become the focus of many ecumenical debates about ministry and ordination, highlighting underlying theological debates about ordination in Church life. These underlying discussions are particularly important in a contemporary context where many churches (especially in the West) are facing decreased membership and funds. In this context, many churches are seeking to develop wider involvement by the laity in running (as well as participating) in their life and work, whilst being able to employ fewer paid ministers. They are also seeing an increasing diversity of additional specialist roles (such as youth ministers) that do not necessarily fit within traditional role descriptions. These changes are often forcing churches to re-evaluate their traditional understandings of roles in terms of who can contribute and in which ways, as well as how these roles relate to understandings of ordination. Deacons have often found themselves at the centre of these debates, as a role which is explicitly mentioned in the Bible that is neither priest/presbyter nor lay, and also as a role which is often involved in some form of enabling others.

Practically, different denominations have also varied over their understandings of the requirements placed on deacons when they take on this role, and any support which will be provided by the Church to enable deacons to fulfil their duties. Together, these understandings of role, status, support and organisation have adapted flexibly over time to a wide range of different situations and contexts, taking on a diverse range of contemporary combinations and forms around the world.[24]

Underlying these different historical practices, Church debates about the diaconate have been reinvigorated by different critical interpretations of Biblical source material in the New Testament related to this role (particularly "diakonia" and its related terms).[25] These critical interpretations have particularly challenged the emphasis within traditional interpretations on "menial service", supporting alternative connotations of "ambassadorial representation"/being a "go-between".[26]

This "go-between" role has often proved to be another reason that diaconal movements have found themselves and their practice to be the focus for controversies, both outside and inside the Church. As those involved in diaconal ministries have engaged in service in the contemporary context, they have represented Christian perspectives through their words and actions in the increasingly diverse context of wider public life discussed earlier. This has put them at the centre of debates concerning how the Church should engage in the contested territory created by broader challenges to the relationship between faith and civil society noted at the start of this introduction. It has particularly placed them in the middle of debates over whether, how and when to speak of their faith when working with people who may be considered vulnerable.

These reinvigorated diaconal movements have often also found themselves in the midst of churches' wider responses to the highly political social issues of global economic injustice and marginalisation.[27] Indeed, some have argued that the nature of diaconal ministry lies precisely in being "de-centred" ministry, working with the "outsider" and on the margins, to challenge this exclusion.[28] This contribution has often been highly controversial when it has involved radical offers of service to those who are outcast and providing advocacy on behalf of those with less power, seeking opportunities to engage in transformative practices for social care and social justice. Moreover, diaconal ministries have often not just sought to do this *on behalf of* disadvantaged groups, but also sought to involve groups who have been discriminated against *within ministry to others*. This involvement of disadvantaged groups in ministry has also been highly controversial when it has challenged prejudice in the Church and wider society, not least historically where it has created new opportunities for women to take on recognised ministries in the public sphere.

As a church-authorised ministry in an increasingly professionalised world, the diaconate has also faced significant questions about how their ministry relates to understandings of "good practice" in related professional roles such as social work, nursing, community work and youth work. Whilst diaconal ministries historically contributed towards the original development of these related professions, since then, increasing specialisation, professionalisation and regulation, as well as changing Church expectations, have changed this relationship. This has led to contemporary debates in different countries about what role, if any, should be played by faith in general, and deacons in particular, in the work of these professions today.

Those engaged in diaconal ministries perform a role within the Church that continues to operate at this interface between the Church and the wider social context. As such, their critical reflection on their experiences has significant potential to help the Church learn how to respond to these contemporary challenges of wider social engagement.[29] Indeed, these challenges of engagement and ministry are embodied in deacons' everyday work, and reflect issues which are central to the Church's mission, life, purpose and future within this context. Hence, by studying the everyday understandings of deacons in one denomination, and the challenges they face within their ministry, this book critically explores what these experiences can tell us about making connections between the Christian faith, churches and wider communities within the contemporary context. In addition, by exploring tensions within understandings of ministry arising from deacons' experiences within this denomination, it highlights opportunities for learning how the Church might become more effective in enabling all Christian believers to live out their faith with integrity in their everyday lives.

1.2.   THE CONTRIBUTION OF THIS BOOK

This book explores deacons' experiences of this role within the Methodist Church in Britain.[30] A deacon's primary purpose is understood by this denomination to be the provision of a focus for the "servant ministry" of the whole Church. Their role is seen as providing witness through service in ways that represent, model and enable this servant ministry in the Church and wider community.[31] The ordination promises made by these deacons commit them in God's name:

> To assist God's people in worship and prayer;
> to hold before them the needs and concerns of the world;
> to minister Christ's love and compassion;
> to visit and support the sick and the suffering;
> to seek out the lost and the lonely;
> and to help those you serve to offer their lives to God.
> Fulfil your calling as disciples of Jesus Christ, who came not to be served but to serve.
> In all things, give counsel and encouragement to all whom Christ entrusts to your care.
> Pray without ceasing.
> Work with joy in the Lord's service.
> Let no one suffer hurt through your neglect.[32]

Since 1998, both men and women have been able to become Methodist deacons in Britain, becoming ordained to a full time, life-long order of ministry following these promises. Within this ministry, they have also been part of a dispersed religious order (the Methodist Diaconal Order). The roots of this Methodist Diaconal Order lie in the Wesley Deaconess Order, through which women had previously ministered for around 100 years.[33] Those belonging to the Methodist Diaconal Order are sent (through a "stationing" process) to locally funded positions wherever the national Methodist Church ("the Connexion") wishes to send them. Many of these positions are within a ministry team within a group of local Methodist churches ("a Circuit"). As ministers within the Methodist Church, they receive a financial stipend and housing, on terms which are now the same as those of the other order of ministry (presbyters) recognised within this denomination. Deacons within the Methodist Diaconal Order follow a common "Rule of Life" which provides a framework for their collective devotional life and discipline.[34]

This book is based on detailed research carried out over two years with deacons belonging to this Methodist Diaconal Order.[35] It seeks to offer a reflective narrative on diaconal ministry, as expressed by the deacons whom this Church has ordained to be a focus and representative form of it.[36] This narrative arose from a thorough investigative process that sought to engage a wide range of Methodist deacons in collective practical theological reflection on this ministry. The research process invited deacons to reflect critically together on examples of what they would consider to be "good practice" within their ministry. It then explored, collated and analysed the resulting discourses in light of wider literature, together with data gathered from a range of supporting methods. The aim was not to produce one "ideal model" of diaconal ministry, but to encourage dialogue about the underlying (often implicit) understandings, theologies and value judgements that were being used within it. By beginning to explore some of these in a more explicit way, the research aimed to resource further reflection and dialogue between different deacons, and between deacons and the wider Church, as they develop their understanding and practice of this ministry together. As with all ministries within the Church, deacons' ministries take place in a wider context. Because of this, the research process also involved some additional activities which began to place the deacons' perspectives in this wider context.[37]

By engaging in robust practical theological research drawing together these reflections, this investigation aimed to address a gap in empirical research on the challenges and opportunities of the contemporary deacon's role. This report seeks to reflect faithfully Methodist deacons' diverse perspectives, whilst analysing how they might fit together. Chapter 2 reflects on this diversity, and how it might be acknowledged within the development of a shared underlying understanding of their ministry.

Chapter 3 explores how deacons' ministries often seek to find ways to discern and make connections between presence, service, witness, enabling others and developing the Church in ethical ways. A key part of this is the way in which diaconal practice raises crucial issues concerning how the Church engages with, and responds to, people in wider society; especially those who are marginalised. This leads on to Chapter 4, which explores the way that making connections within and between churches and wider communities is central to a deacon's role. Chapter 5 considers deacons' understanding of how *their own identities* contributed to their ability to make these connections. As is explored in Chapter 6, this material provokes helpful reflections on the relationships between the Church's mission and different understandings of ministry, including the relationships between ministries, both lay and ordained. It also highlights the continuing effects of the Church's history, especially over controversial issues such as the relationship between gender and ministry. The book concludes in Chapter 7 by exploring the extent to which learning is currently being shared from deacons' individual experiences, including the opportunities and challenges they face in their ministry, and how the effectiveness of learning exchanges between deacons, and between deacons and others, might be improved.

With all research, there are always further perspectives that could be included in order to gain a more comprehensive picture. This is especially important to note in the case of this work, in which perspectives from others in the Church, and those with whom deacons work in wider society, could all helpfully add to (and perhaps challenge) the picture painted here. In this spirit, the book offers key theological questions linked to each chapter. These questions arise from reflecting on the perspectives shared. They are intended to encourage further critical consideration of these findings not only by deacons, but also by those supporting them in their learning and development, and by the wider Church. These questions by themselves do not necessarily claim to be new insights; indeed, it is envisaged that a wide range of existing theological, theoretical and practical resources could helpfully be drawn on in responding to them. However, by highlighting their collective importance, and considering how they relate together within empirical research on deacons' ministries in this context, new insights can emerge which have the potential to improve understanding and practice. These questions have arisen within the context of the Methodist Church in Britain, which has its own history, polity and theological emphases that may not be shared by all denominations. However, there is evidence from the ecumenical conversations engaged in throughout the research[38] that many of the underlying issues resonate with the experiences of other denominations, albeit sometimes in different ways. By seeking to reflect faithfully Methodist deacons' diverse perspectives, their experience is offered up for wider discussion, comparison and reflection by those in other traditions, as well as within their own. The authors hope that these questions will support continuing constructive conversations and indicate helpful directions for the development of future work that further develop this ministry's important contribution to the wider Church and society within the challenging context outlined.

NOTES

1. The debates in this section are explored in more detail in Orton 2012.
2. Morisy 2009.
3. On the contribution of religious organisations to social welfare in Europe, for example, see Bäckström et al. 2010.
4. See, for example, Davie 2007.
5. Furbey 2009, pp. 21–40. For one author's particularly relevant critique of Christianity's traditional mode of operation in relation to this, see Clark 2005.
6. Bosch 1991.
7. Morisy 2004.
8. Avis 2009, pp. 3–6.
9. Barnett 1981.
10. Renewed Diaconate Working Party of the House of Bishops 2001.
11. Avis 2009, p. 3.
12. World Council of Churches 1982, p. 24.
13. Ibid.
14. Ibid.
15. For an outline of the range of roles in different denominations, see, for example: Avis 2005, especially pp. 103–114; Diocese of Salisbury 2003, especially pp. 48–56.
16. See, for example, Staton 2001.
17. Following the practice of the Methodist Church in Britain, which is the primary focus of this book, the term "deacon" is generally used to refer to both men and women, except where qualified by a particular gendered description.

"Deaconess" is only used in historical reference where this was the correct description at the time.

18. See, for example, the various descriptions of how these services developed in different European countries in Bäckström et al. 2010.

19. See Bäckström et al. 2010. For a related study in the USA, also see Wittberg 2006.

20. Barnett 1981; Avis 2005.

21. For example, see Diocese of Salisbury 2003; also Barnett 1981. This was also recognised as a strong emerging trend as far back as World Council of Churches 1982, p. 24.

22. See, for example, accounts of the way that gender has historically impacted on these debates within the Church of England represented in Francis 1999; Grierson 1981.

23. World Council of Churches 1982, p. 24.

24. Diakonia World Federation Executive Committee 1998; Renewed Diaconate Working Party of the House of Bishops 2001. This variety of understandings continues to be represented in the Diakonia World Federation membership today.

25. Gooder 2008, pp. 99–108. For a critical historical analysis of how these developing interpretations influenced the Reformed tradition in its development of diaconal ministry, see Latvus 2010, pp. 82–102.

26. Gooder 2006, pp. 33–56; Collins 2009, pp. 69–81.

27. World Council of Churches 2012.

28. McRae 2009.

29. World Council of Churches 1982; Clark 2008. A fuller and more widely-referenced analysis of the global debates highlighted in this section, and the location of the Methodist Diaconal Order within them, is provided in Orton 2012.

30. For the sake of this report, from here onwards all references to "The Methodist Church" in this report refer to the Methodist Church in Britain, which is the focus of this study. (Other Methodist traditions differ in various ways, and the views of deacons in these churches were outside the scope of this study.) Its founding document, the Deed of Union of the Methodist Church in Britain, states that "The Methodist Church claims and cherishes its place in the Holy Catholic Church which is the Body of Christ". Hence following common usage, the capitalised term "Church" refers in an inclusive way to this universal global Church, irrespective of denomination, unless a particular denomination is stated at the time. In contrast, the un-capitalised term "church" refers to a particular local congregation.

31. Methodist Church in Britain 2004.

32. Methodist Church in Britain 1999, p. 317.

33. The Wesley Deaconess Order was founded in 1890, within a historical context which included other Methodist deaconess movements founded at a similar time; see Staton 2001 and Graham 2002 for a fuller history. Sections 6.3.3 and 6.3.4 below give further details of this development and its contemporary impact on the Methodist Diaconal Order.

34. For a copy of the "Rule of Life", please see Appendix D.

35. Full details of this approach, the methods used and the broader methodological framework are detailed in Appendix A.

36. Cf. Methodist Church in Britain 2004.

37. These activities are also detailed in Appendix A.

38. As detailed in Appendices A and C.

2. EXPLORING CONTEMPORARY PERSPECTIVES: AN INTRODUCTION

2.1. DIVERSITY AND FLEXIBILITY: RESPONDING TO NEED AND CONTEXT

The research began by asking deacons to reflect on examples of "good practice" within their own ministry.[1] When asking any particular group of deacons to share examples of good practice from their ministry, the first impression gained was the remarkable diversity of activities in which they were involved. Deacons[2] gave accounts of ministry encounters that took place in a **wide range of settings**, including hospitals and prisons, local estates and international airports, homes and streets, community shops and night shelters, and churches and schools. Deacons also spoke of their efforts to come alongside a very **diverse range of people**. These included young people, bereaved mothers, civil servants, asylum seekers, local sex workers, those dependent on drugs or alcohol, those suffering from Alzheimer's disease, and those who were perceived to be disconnected from or on the margins of churches and communities (to highlight just a small sample). Their descriptions of their work also encompassed a **wide range of potential objectives**: from the unmistakably evangelistic activities of leading an Alpha course or working with a church that had been recently planted in a new housing estate, to the more indefinite practice of "just drinking a cup of coffee" with someone.

Indeed, the deacons interviewed for this research repeatedly emphasised how difficult it was to summarise what deacons do with any level of precision, especially given the apparently dissimilar activities in which they are engaged. One deacon outlined this difficulty well, asserting that "each of us has a very different role in a different way."[3]

She continued by saying:

> [That] is why it is so difficult to sit down and say, you know, "this is a typical deacon", because it will be . . . [different] for every single one of us. There [are] no two that you could write the same sentence for.
>
> **Respondent, *Area Group D***

Part of the reason for this was considered to be the range of individual differences between deacons:

> Different deacons have such different roles and gifts and skills that they bring, and valid callings, and you know, what is it that God's calling us to be and do?
>
> **Respondent, *Area Group G***

This diversity within the outward form of deacons' ministries was seen by many deacons as having arisen in response to the different needs of particular Circuits[4] and communities in different times and contexts. As one deacon suggested:

> When we are stationed and when we go to a Circuit they are asking for particular things of the deacon—which is why you will find as you go around that deacons will do different things.
>
> **Respondent, *Area Group M***

This deacon went on to state that although some deacons will work with refugees, some with young people, and others in pastoral contexts with older people, what ultimately determines the type of work done is the need of the Circuit:

> They [the Circuit] have identified a need and a specific work to do within the Circuit and that's why you find so much diversity and so many different roles of the deacon because we have been asked to do different things.

Having diverse deacons with diverse gifts, available to be stationed to various Circuits and contexts for ministry with different needs, was seen as providing the wider Church with a considerable resource, in which this diversity is a substantial strength. By making themselves and their gifts available to the wider Church, deacons allowed the Methodist Church, through its stationing process, to seek to match the character and gifts of particular individuals to the needs of particular Circuits and contexts. The structure of the Methodist Diaconal Order provided (amongst other things) a framework within which the particularly diverse contributions offered by deacons could be co-ordinated, balanced and developed in response to the needs of the wider Church.

Many deacons also saw themselves as needing to adapt flexibly as individuals to the diverse contexts in which they were placed by the wider Methodist Church's "stationing" process, as part of their itinerant ministry.[5] As they moved, they then had to navigate changing roles for themselves which fitted with the different requirements of particular places. As deacons found themselves in different settings, many argued that flexibility was essential to meet the changing needs of the post. This involved continually negotiating their roles with others within that particular space. One interviewee articulated the importance of this flexibility well:

> This is what we must do, be open for whatever we have to do and change and fit into that situation and get on with the job. I mean that's been one of our things, hasn't it? That we've always said we are flexible to whatever the church needs, never mind whether you can explain it or put it in a box.
>
> **Respondent, *Area Group N***

This flexibility has developed as a crucial characteristic of deacons, in response to changing needs throughout the history of the Methodist Diaconal Order and the Wesley Deaconess Order.[6] In this context, deacons sought to adapt to these changing needs within the Methodist Church and wider society. However, in analysing the data, it became clear that all this diversity in outward forms of practice had also created difficulties for deacons collectively, by making it difficult for deacons to explain to others what was at the heart of all they did. Deacons had found that it was equally difficult for others within the Church, who saw what appeared to be very different examples of deacons' ministries, to understand what existed in common between all deacons' roles. This was also set within a historical context in which the contributions required of deacons by the wider Church, and their relationship to other ministries, had changed and developed over time.[7] As a result, deacons' flexibility and diversity of roles in different times and places—coupled with the diversity of their gifts and characters—resulted in a high degree of ambiguity surrounding deacons and their practice. Deacons expressed considerable frustration with continually having to explain to others who deacons were and what deacons did, particularly to others within the Church. They recounted numerous incidents of encounters with people within local churches who had a limited understanding of the Methodist Church's official position on *What is a Deacon?*[8] Many deacons also felt that their existing explanations were frequently misunderstood, and that these misunderstandings operated on several levels, as will be considered below. These deacons felt that there was a need to articulate more clearly the nature of their ministry, and to communicate and educate the wider Church about the contribution that their ministry can make. Some recognised that they hadn't always been good at communicating the understanding behind their work to others, particularly in writing more theoretically. For example, one experienced deacon who regularly talked with others about different forms of deacons' ministries commented:

> The problem is we wouldn't write about [a deacon's ministry] in the same academic way … [a colleague] keeps saying to me … that I need to write it down … but neither of us are the sort who would write it down, so we've decided we need a conversation with someone who *can* write it down.

However, some deacons resisted attempts to try to define too closely what their ministry entailed, as they felt that this could not, or should not, be done. For example, one deacon commented:

> Just by the fact that you are trying to tightly define it means that you are going to miss part of it anyway.
>
> **Respondent,** *Area Group R*

These deacons saw their role as having an inherent creativity that resisted neat categorisation. For example, one deacon recalled a Circuit treasurer's confusion when faced with how to account for a creative piece of work in which the deacon had been involved. The treasurer asked, "Well, what column do I put that under?" When the deacon sought to clarify this request by asking what was meant, the treasurer responded, "Well, I haven't got a column for this sort of thing!" For the deacons discussing this situation, this lack of a column in the financial accounts was a good example of the way that churches could get stuck seeing themselves in particular ways, and miss those activities which did not fit into traditional categories. In response to situations like this, deacons frequently engaged in creative discussions with those in churches about how those churches currently understood their mission and existing activities. This enabled them to provoke reflection on how these churches might grow further in their understanding of God's mission, including engaging in more flexible ways of thinking about their ministries, even when the resulting work didn't fit within traditional categories or columns.

These deacons were particularly concerned that any functionalist definition of their ministry (in terms of what they did or did not do) would miss the essence of what they were about, which was embedded in *who they were*. As will be discussed further in Chapter 5, these deacons were amongst those who felt that it was important to focus on their "being" rather than "doing". Furthermore, it was through this way of being that deacons saw themselves as breaking down many of the boundaries which might otherwise inhibit the Church's mission.

KEY QUESTIONS

1. In what ways is the diversity of deacons' ministries helpful to the wider Church?
2. Are there any ways in which this diversity can be problematic for the wider Church?
3. Can particular ministries be described or defined in ways that distinguish them without undermining their ability to be creative and flexible in practice? If so, what approaches or ways of doing this are most helpful?

2.2.   DIMENSIONS OF GOOD PRACTICE

The research process sought to engage with this diverse, flexible and creative character of ministry and bring together deacons' different experiences in dialogue with each other. Despite some deacons' reservations about over-defining a deacon's role, a clearer shared picture began to develop as deacons explored their examples of what they considered to be "good practice" within their ministry. What emerged from this process was a clear sense that deacons understood good practice to be something that understands, connects and integrates a whole range of different factors or dimensions in their ministry. These various dimensions, which are brought together in a particular deacon's daily life, through their identity and encounters, included:

1. **What diaconal ministry seeks to do**, focusing particularly on its aims, purposes and its underpinning theology.
2. **How deacons go about doing it**—specifically, the day-to-day process and practice of ministry within a particular context.
3. **The connections and relationships formed** with (and between) different individuals, groups and organisations that are involved within a particular context, that develop as a result of diaconal ministry.
4. **Who deacons are**—involving aspects such as their personal motivations, their character, their spiritual life and their individual circumstances.
5. **What deacons offer**—such as their availability, life-long commitment and the willingness to be stationed where sent.

Importantly, these five dimensions connected together in a highly integrated way in which each dimension relied on the others. Thus, the way in which the practice is carried out and the person carrying it out are just as much an essential part of the ministry as its intentions and aims. To understand properly the integrated nature of good practice, it is essential to recognise these different dimensions, and the relationship between them, and not confuse one dimension with another.

Recognising their integration, we now turn towards an examination of each of these dimensions. *"What diaconal ministry seeks to do"* and *"how deacons go about doing it"* will be addressed first in Chapter 3, which looks at the day-to-day processes and purposes of a deacon's ministry. Chapter 4 then goes on to explore *"the connections and relationships . . . that develop as a result of this diaconal ministry"*. *"Who deacons are"*, *"What deacons offer"*, and the relationships between deacons' ministries and the ministries of others will then be explored. These are covered in Chapter 5, Chapter 6 and the beginning of Chapter 7 (up to and including Section 7.2). Finally, the remainder of the book from Section 7.3 onwards will explore how deacons develop their understandings of their ministry, and how they might continue to develop this understanding in dialogue with others.

NOTES

1. For further details of this process and how the concept of "good practice" was used to stimulate a critically reflective research process, see Appendix A.

2. Throughout this book, unless otherwise stated, the term "deacon" has been used inclusively to include those who are ordained deacons, probationer deacons and student deacons within the Methodist Church in Britain.

3. Please see the methodological discussion in Appendix A for further details of the ways in which quotations are used throughout this book. In particular, please note that the inclusion of a quotation in one particular voice does not necessarily mean that the authors, other deacons or the Methodist Diaconal Order collectively would necessarily agree with the comment, or the particular way it has been phrased. All quotations are cited as spoken, which means that (like most speech) they are not always quite grammatically correct. Where it helps to clarify the meaning, minor alterations have been made. Following common conventions, in all places where these have been made, the alterations are indicated by [text in square brackets] within the quote. Where words have been cut from the quote for the same purpose, this is indicated by " . . . ".

4. In the Methodist Church in Britain, a "Circuit" is a group of local congregations which work together in a local area as part of the national Methodist Church, known as the "Connexion". Both presbyters and deacons are appointed to particular Circuits by the Methodist Conference through a "stationing process", whereby those presbyters and deacons available to be placed are matched with vacant positions.

5. As noted previously, both presbyters and deacons in the Methodist Church are placed through this stationing process. These processes and their implications

share much in common, whilst retaining some differences. These differences have included a greater historical expectation that deacons should go where they are first sent ("direct stationing"), with less room to express their views about which particular appointment they are allocated. See Section 6.3.3 for further analysis of this.

6. These changing requirements of the Church concerning what they wanted from their deacons were very clear in the empirical accounts, and also supported by related studies; see, for example, Staton 2001; Graham 2002.

7. See Chapter 6.

8. Methodist Church in Britain 2004.

3. PROCESSES OF GOOD PRACTICE IN DIACONAL MINISTRY

3.1. INTRODUCTION TO CHAPTER 3

As deacons began sharing diverse descriptions of their practice, a remarkably consistent set of themes emerged when describing the particular way in which they went about their ministry. In fact, *how deacons went about their practice* was central to their understanding of what made particular practice "good". These processes within their ministry began with four key ways in which they saw themselves as forming relationships: through **presence**, **service**, **discernment**, and **witness**. In this third chapter, each of these aspects will be considered in turn. Moreover, out of the developing conversations and analysis arising from the research, it became clear that deacons saw as a key purpose of their ministry the establishment of ways to make connections between these four aspects.

However, there remained some important debates about how these aspects of ministry might relate to each other, as this third chapter will also explore. In addition, as we will explore further in Section 3.2.5 and Chapter 6, many deacons recognised that others were also involved in doing things in this way. Indeed, one of a deacon's primary callings is to support and enable others to engage in these processes and make these connections for themselves, not just rely on deacons to do it for them. As a result, it is important to state here at the outset that deacons' claim of a "diaconal way" of doing things were not exclusive claims (that "only deacons do things this way"). Instead, it was an inclusive one, and one that starts (as in the Methodist Church's 2004 statement *What is a Deacon?*[1]) with a particular approach to the calling of the whole Church:

> The starting point must therefore be the calling of all God's people
> to share in the work of worship, mission and service, both before

God and in the world. The particular ministries of presbyters and
deacons can only be understood within this context, as focusing,
expressing and enabling the ministry of the whole people of God.
All such ministry is, as the word implies, *service*: service to God in
service to the church and the world. Thus, servant ministry is the
task and calling of the whole people of God as they seek to continue
the work of Christ in the power of the Holy Spirit; taking Christ
as pattern and inspiration: "I am among you as one who serves"
(Lk. 22.27).[2]

In this sense, we found it increasingly helpful to distinguish carefully
between our use of the terms "diaconal" and "deacon" when undertaking
the analysis of the research data, in the sense that:

> *Deacons do diaconal ministry (and indeed provide a particular focus
> for it)—but that doesn't mean that all diaconal ministry is done by
> deacons.*

Neither does this mean that diaconal ministry can *only* be understood
through understanding the ministry of deacons. Nevertheless, reflecting
on deacons' understandings is pertinent, as they are the people whom the
Church has collectively called to focus and represent this wider calling of
diaconal ministry to themselves and others.[3]

As deacons sought to hold these understandings in conjunction with
each other, a fifth aspect emerged which was central to their understandings
of good practice within their own ministry. The four aspects of presence,
service, discernment, and witness described above were underpinned by
an additional important dimension to their ministry: that deacons sought
to **enable, encourage and equip others** to be involved within these aspects
of diaconal ministry. This book will return to explore these issues more
thoroughly later.[4]

Through the process of collective theological reflection stimulated
by the group discussions with deacons, ways were sought to describe
the purpose of doing all these things. In this, the adjective "missional"
was found by the researchers to be a potentially helpful addition to
the deacons' terms "presence", "service", "discernment" and "witness".
Whilst the adjective "missional" was rarely used by deacons at the outset
when describing particular practice examples, it frequently emerged in

subsequent discussions as a helpful concept when exploring different understandings of each of these aspects. The wide range of important debates over how mission should be understood, and how churches should apply the resulting understandings within their contemporary life, formed an important dimension to this discussion. Crucially, this term also captured many of the important debates that emerged over how these different aspects of diaconal ministry might be connected, and what the purposes might be for deacons in making these connections. When it was included in the discussions, it helped to ground them within a wider recognition that diaconal ministry contributes to the central purpose of the whole Church as it seeks to participate in God's mission.[5] In addition, it reflected a description on a recent publicity booklet in which the Methodist Diaconal Order describes itself as "a mission-focused, pioneering religious community committed to enabling outreach, evangelism and service in God's world."[6]

3.2.   PROCESSES OF GOOD PRACTICE

This section considers in turn the aspects of **presence, service, discernment, witness** and **enabling/encouraging others** which were found to be key themes within deacons' accounts of their practice. Through this discussion, it becomes apparent that debates about good practice in diaconal ministry centre on the relationships and connections which arise from and between these different ways of engaging with others. In particular, deacons' examples of good practice frequently centre on how they sought to find creative ways to form and model relationships that connected these different aspects. Their challenges and dilemmas also regularly arise from the interactions between these aspects of their ministry.

3.2.1.   Missional Presence

As deacons described what they did, they placed considerable stress on the notion of *presence*, and this feature of their ministry emerged as an essential component in their understanding of good practice. Indeed, this theme was present in all twenty-two area group interviews. Deacons repeatedly used phrases such as "being there", "coming alongside", "being available", "being with", "listening", "talking", and "building relationships" to articulate the fundamental aspects of their ministry.

These aspects of presence formed an essential starting place for a deacon's ministry, with this theme occurring in every area group discussion. As these quotations illustrate, this presence was not just passive; it involved an active process of forming relationships. This began by connecting with people, and building relationships with them by starting wherever they were at the time. Indeed, deacons saw their ministry as fundamentally relational, as the following quotations illustrate:

> The relationships have to be there first.
>
> **Respondent,** *Area Group B*

> It's about relationship and building relationships.
>
> **Respondent,** *Area Group M*

> It's been crucial for me to be alongside people and to be building relationships with people.
>
> **Respondent,** *Area Group N*

> There is something beautiful about human relationship and that for me is about where the transformation takes place.
>
> **Respondent,** *Area Group A*

The deacon's presence, availability and time were all seen as a significant pre-requisite for enabling these relationships to be developed. Deacons recognised that they could play a purposive role in creating the potential for these relationships to emerge. As this section will now consider in more detail, they did this through strategies such as finding time to be available for others, recognising the importance of time in allowing a process of relationship-building to develop, and creating spaces where people could linger.

The element of time factored into deacons' understandings in a range of different ways. Firstly, deacons repeatedly recognized that **their availability and time arose because they had been "freed up"** by the Methodist Church from other responsibilities, and were immensely grateful to the wider Church for enabling this to happen. This meant that they had the time needed to make themselves available and through this could offer the time needed to build up these important relationships with others. For example, when asked to reflect on what their examples of good practice had in common, different deacons in one area group responded with the following flurry of words:

> Listening seems an important thing.
> And time.
> Availability.
> Understanding.
> It's "travelling with" to a certain degree, isn't it?
> Selflessness.
>
> **Various respondents,** *Area Group U*

For the deacons concerned, these words were also connected to each other. It was not just their availability and listening that was important, but also the opportunities that this created (such as opportunities for "travelling with" people and understanding them). It was also about how their presence was combined with a particular attitude (such as "selflessness") through which the deacons were able to show an orientation to the needs of others. Deacons saw this as requiring both "an openness to people" and "reaching out" to them; both "coming alongside" people and "not just waiting for them to come to you: go and look for them—the lost and the lonely."

Secondly, many of the examples of good diaconal practice started with finding or **creating times and spaces for other people to linger.** For example, many deacons indicated that this could often involve something as simple as just having a cup of coffee with someone. (An illustration of the importance ascribed by deacons to the opportunities this afforded was the frequency with which cups of tea or coffee were mentioned in the interviews—cumulatively 59 times in total!)

> I see the deacon as being there, just being available as much as anything. Not rushing off busy . . . don't let that person see that you are busy. Make it appear that you have got all the time in the world.
>
> **Respondent,** *Area Group D*

From their presence in a particular physical place, deacons were involved in creating safe spaces for people to interact with them and with each other. For example, one deacon talked about a particular opportunity for interaction that they had established:

> An example of being available . . . to enable and facilitate something I feel is still growing is [an art group we've started]. I'd like to define it as creating safe space for people to be creative and for those others who volunteer to be Christ [in] getting alongside people. It's been running for over a year now.
>
> **Respondent, *Area Group U***

Another deacon talked about how she had used a manse for a similar purpose, as a place where people could meet and interact on the local estate:

> I was asked to live here. This was not what I chose or somewhere within the community development, but I thought, "well, this a substantial house, how can we use it?" So to provide the space for people to gather in small groups, and be confident enough to do that, with exploring their own way of being in the world through creativity—to a lesser or greater extent. And it's just an absolute gift and privilege to be able to have this space, the physical space, as a deacon to be able to do that. And it seems so natural to provide a peaceful place and comfortable place with some food and just to be.
>
> **Respondent, *Area Group S***

Nevertheless, the aspects of diaconal practice that relate to time and presence often raise questions about **what it is that deacons actually *do* when they are present** and taking this time. Some deacons indicated that others have sometimes perceived them as not really doing anything except being present. Yet, the analysis found that many deacons have a clear sense of the spiritual implications of their presence. One interviewee in particular captured this dynamic when describing the importance of presence and taking time in chaplaincy work:

> I think that this is very, very important to all of us. It's very easy to get caught up in "what do you do, how are you filling in your time, are you at a meeting, are you doing this, this, this and this" and it's

not about that. It's being available and quite often people may think that you are wasting your time. You know they might think "what's she doing there having a cup of coffee and just . . . she's not doing anything!" And they kind of don't get it that that's what it's about, it's being available for people and listening and that's what it's about. One of the things that I do is going to [a local supermarket] as their Chaplain and sometimes I wander around and the staff are all busy, you know they are all at the checkouts, but as I wander around I can be lifting them to God in prayer and when they have got a quiet moment I can just come alongside and see how their day is going.

Respondent, *Area Group U*

Many deacons also had a deep sense of the inherent potential within their unconditional presence and availability. When describing the importance of their presence, deacons would often cite the ministerial or pastoral opportunities that arose as a result of time spent with others. This gave a clear indication that the creation of these opportunities provided a key purpose that lay behind practices such as these. However, deacons recognized that this process "takes a long time", and it was seen as important not to rush this. This was because it was important that the presence was offered unconditionally, so it required a considerable amount of time for the "seeds planted" through their presence to grow and bear fruit in terms of the creation of those opportunities when people wished to engage with them.

These opportunities for ministry arose not just because of deacons' physical presence and the time they spent, but also because of the particular position that they took in being present. Indeed, as one deacon expressed it:

We talk about presence, but it's presence as a deacon, not just any old presence, but it's presence as a deacon and representative of the Church.

Respondent, *Area Group E*

Similarly, another interviewee stressed how, in her ministry to those addicted to alcohol, she did not "sit alongside them as another alcoholic. I sit alongside them as [one] who is a deacon in the Methodist Church. So I don't have a neutral stance" (Respondent, *Area Group A).*

These quotations illustrate two key findings also present within the wider data which were important in understanding the nature of the presence offered by deacons. Firstly, deacons managed their encounters best when they were reflexively aware of what they represented through their presence in a particular situation as a deacon. In being present and available to form relationships in particular situations, the presence of the deacon as a representative of the Church often has symbolic as well as practical significance; for example, by showing visible solidarity with people that some others might avoid. These issues of a deacon's identity and its relationship with presence and purpose are considered further in Chapter 5.

Secondly, these quotations helpfully begin to highlight debates over what the deacons' purposes are in offering this presence. For example, one experienced deacon who saw their own role as "just being available" nevertheless jokily described the importance of lingering to make yourself available to others as "loitering with intent". The use of the particular phrase "loitering with intent" was especially controversial, as for some it held highly unhelpful and inappropriate connotations of association with criminal behaviour. Whether the particular phrase was used or not, related debates nevertheless highlighted the importance of being clear what deacons' intentions may be. Some deacons saw this intent as being simply to engage with whoever or whatever situation turned up. However, many recognised that their role was necessarily more intentional than this over the longer term, and sought to engage in more positive ways that the subsequent sections in this chapter will explore. Key intentions proposed by the deacons for their engagement included offering service, engaging in missional discernment, seeking opportunities to witness, and building relationships across communities. In turn, these debates raised questions over whether these different intentions could be combined, and if so, how this might be done ethically in ways that corresponded with their own and the Church's theological understandings of the nature of the Gospel. Underlying all these debates, the importance of the unconditional nature of a deacon's presence and availability to enter into relationships was a common theme which was fundamental to many deacons' understandings of their ministry.[7]

All this evidence points to the way that deacons saw presence as a crucial element of good practice in diaconal ministry. However, it also highlights how understandings of presence alone were not sufficient to constitute a holistic understanding of good practice. Indeed, reflecting on the way that this presence related to other understandings of a deacon's purpose and identity was crucial to realising its potential.

3.2.2.   Missional Service

Many churches have traditionally understood deacons' ministries primarily in terms of service.[8] Alongside presence, the concept of service was also central to the understanding of good practice expressed by the deacons in the research, with this concept appearing in all 22 area group interviews. Deacons frequently used the language of "service" and "serving" in their explanations of their practice. For example, one deacon explained why she believed her task in a particular situation had been diaconal by responding "Well, because it's service!" (Respondent, *Area Group G*). Another deacon saw the key to understanding good practice in diaconal ministry as being about asking "What does it mean to be a servant in this place?" (Respondent, *Area Group M*). They also frequently gave descriptions of actual encounters where they had embodied this concept by responding to need, caring for others, and supporting those on the margins.[9] For example, one deacon described the purpose of diaconal ministry as being to offer "love and care, caring about those that perhaps other people don't care about" (Respondent, *Area Group U*).

Importantly, there were both responsive and proactive elements to a deacon's service. Some interviewees spoke about responding to need as it was presented to them. For example, one claimed that a deacon's practice is "about looking and seeing and searching and being able to say 'Yes, I'll do that!'" (Respondent, *Area Group A*). Others spoke of actively "seeking out the lost and the lonely", referring to one phrase in their ordination promises. By providing unconditional service, even where they didn't directly speak the Gospel, deacons saw themselves as responding to needs in practical ways. They also saw themselves as retaining vital spiritual dimensions to their service by embodying and enacting the Gospel in a tangible form through the process of serving:

> It's about meeting a need where it is and it's an embodiment of putting oil on somebody's head when you greet them, feeding them when they are hungry, visiting them, washing them, do you know

what I mean? So it's an embodiment of that Gospel imperative to serve where needed, and there is need there.

Respondent, *Area Group L*

Whether it be in the workplace, whether it be in older people's homes or behind closed doors in private homes where people are struggling, you know it's the need aspect, it's the seeking out the lost and the lonely, and approaching that in practical ways that's completely underpinned by the Gospel and prayer

Respondent, *Area Group T*

One deacon spoke particularly about the expectations of deacons as ordained ministers to embody this notion of service and consciously model it to others, even in difficult situations:

I suppose the bottom line is "what it is to be a servant?" I'm stating the obvious, but what does it mean to be a servant? And somebody was asking what difference does it make being ordained, but actually I realise it does make a difference being a deacon. There are certain things about being a servant that I can't get away with, like when there was a big misunderstanding at a local church. I could have walked away, but actually God was calling me as a servant to actually offer an apology and to actually do some sort of reconciliation. But if I hadn't, if I wasn't a deacon, [I might have walked away without apologising.] . . . I'm not trying to put deacons on a pedestal . . . but actually the thing about being a servant is that you don't walk away, you offer a model of ministry for all. That's what God requires of us.

Respondent, *Area Group M*

However, many deacons also reflected critically together on what type of service they were called to offer, noting that offering service did not necessarily mean "being a doormat" that others could just walk over. Some quoted the The Revd Thomas Bowman Stephenson, a founder of the Order, in terms of offering "service without servility". Others spoke of how they were conscious of wanting to live out an example of being like Jesus, which included both humility and a willingness to challenge others prophetically where necessary.[10]

3.2.3.   Missional Discernment

Missional discernment was the third key theme to emerge from the data concerning good practice in diaconal ministry, appearing in 20 of the 22 area group interviews.

Deacons saw their practice as involving the critical skill of discerning where God was moving in a particular set of circumstances. For instance, one deacon noted the importance of "interpreting where God is in every situation" (Respondent, *Area Group U*). Through this discerning practice, deacons would often alert individuals and congregations to ways in which God might be working in their circumstances, and inviting them to come alongside and participate in this divine mission. One deacon suggested that deacons needed to point people beyond just the human elements of a situation "to point out and say 'well actually, can you track God in this?'" (Respondent, *Area Group B*).

Through this quality of missional discernment, deacons envisioned their ministry as one of "joining up the dots" and helping to open the eyes of others to glimpses of divine grace. This whole process was articulated well by one particular deacon who said:

> I find it really exciting to almost step back and try to see the bigger picture and I call it "joining up the dots", because you see where God is at work. And I always find it interesting that I point it out to people and they've never seen it. But once you alert them to it, then they can see that progression going on.
>
> **Respondent, *Area Group B***

This could involve, for example, getting people to reflect on how their particular church's involvement in a particular project working with vulnerable people had developed over time. In other situations, it might involve spotting that a range of different people were all becoming concerned about a particular social issue. In this situation, the deacon might bring them together to see what they might do about that issue together. An example of this was one deacon who began offering lunch to a range of professionals and volunteers who were all trying in their own way to address issues of human trafficking. Through this, they were able to co-ordinate their efforts, and improve their responses, whilst sharing with each other their motivations for getting involved in these issues.

This practice of seeing the bigger picture of where they believed God was at work had a strong missional dimension to it, as deacons were able to discern and highlight opportunities for particular churches to participate within this mission in particular contexts. This included looking for where they could find God already acting redemptively in the world and seeking to participate in that action.

One aspect of this was coming alongside those who were not members of churches, but who were nevertheless involved in work of a redemptive and restorative nature that for deacons expressed something of God's Kingdom. One deacon described this in the following way:

> I've always sort of seen my role as trying to be part of those that are building the Kingdom community . . . that there are those out there who are not necessarily part of the Church but that I'm out there trying with them in a sort of humble way really, because at times they shame me in terms of what they do to try and feel my way towards what the Kingdom is out there, and the Kingdom is already out there . . . But I think I always see it in a slightly wider way in that how we enable people to understand what it is to be part of the Kingdom community, or they are already that and how we raise their awareness to what's already going on out there.
>
> **Respondent,** *Area Group T*

Clearly this element of a deacon's practice requires a high degree of discernment in identifying where they could see God at work in a given situation, and then making the most of the opportunities this presented. These opportunities included the potential for Christians to get involved in this work, and for them to find ways of pointing others to see God within it.

3.2.4. Missional Witness

As the analysis of deacons' understandings of their practice developed, a fourth theme emerged around the notion of missional witness. This theme was slightly less prevalent than the themes of presence, service and discernment, but still appeared in 16 of the 22 area group interviews. Deacons from a range of these different groups described instances of good practice that involved "trying to get into conversations" about God, "being witnesses to Christ", "sharing and talking about Jesus", and "trying to be Christ in the world".

The analysis also showed that the idea of missional witness in diaconal ministry is about communicating the Gospel in diverse and creative ways. These included articulating the Gospel and also expressing it in other ways; particularly through their actions. This diaconal impulse towards diversity in witness is captured well by an interviewee who remarked:

> I think we're all called, like everybody is called, to communicate the Gospel. Once you've received that salvation, that's the thing that comes with it . . . there's that urge to tell folk. So we're all called to that, and we've all got our distinctive way of doing it, but again, maybe there's something about diaconal ministry . . . I particularly think that diaconal ministry is called to communicate that in as diverse a number of ways as possible.
>
> **Respondent,** *Area Group F*

These diverse and creative ways of witness can be traced through the various processes of presence, service and discernment described above. Accounts similar to this surfaced in the data and represent the inter-related and missional nature of these practices in creating an environment in which the Gospel might be seen and heard. For instance, one deacon noted how presence and service had played important roles in her witness, telling of how she had:

> spent time drinking copious amounts of coffee and digging soil, not physically, but digging over metaphorical soil and planting seeds and slowly dripping bits of Gospel stuff in.
>
> **Respondent,** *Area Group B*

This can often be a gradual and tentative process, as described by the deacon running the art group (mentioned earlier in Section 3.2.1 on "Missional Presence"):

> [The group's] been running for over a year now . . . We are open for teas, coffees, biscuits and people use it as they will . . . sitting round the table in a sort of a circle and telling jokes and having a laugh and singing songs while we are painting . . . We're just starting to

make real connections and we are enjoying being there together
. . . There are hints of God conversations, which are good because
somebody connects slightly with the churches around, so it's just
a work in progress.

Respondent, *Area Group U*

These types of relationships often involved a complex process of discerning
and respectfully negotiating with people within sensitive situations about
when and how it might be considered ethically appropriate to talk of God.
For example, one deacon described working with someone who they felt
had begun to sense God's presence, but who had yet to recognise it. They
talked about:

Trying to get into those conversations to try and understand where
they are coming from and being where they are and trying to help
them understand what that presence is, but not sort of going in with
the God thing straight away, because you can't, can you?

Respondent, *Area Group A*

Three particularly striking examples of this connection between presence,
service and witness came from those deacons working as chaplains:

And of course, the very nature of hospice work means that people
are coming to the end of their lives and that does sharpen up focus
on a lot of things. And so I found that I was put in a very privileged
position many times and I found that quite humbling at times. And
I remember . . . one chap . . . He was a gas engineer, and he was a
bit of a tough cookie, and we'd had quite a few conversations and
I felt as though we hadn't really got anywhere at all. And I went
in to see him one day, and he said, "I've been waiting to see you."
And I said, "Oh, alright". He said, "Sit down, I want to talk to you."
I said, "Fine, OK", and he said, "Now you tell me what's all this
about crucifixion and what does it mean, because I want to know".
And we sort of discussed that and I was there an hour, because he
wouldn't let me go.

Hospice chaplain, *Area Group C*

All my ministry now is chaplaincy, and that ministry is based on presence and relationships. And for me I think that's extremely diaconal in nature, certainly presence, just being there. And in my town centre workplace chaplaincy, I've done six years and it's really come home to me how significant that is in terms of time and building up those relationships. So it's paying off; people who were quite anti are now being connected and talking to me about the deepest things and "can you help me organise my wedding" and "my dad is dying from cancer" and that kind of thing, you know real deep things.

Respondent, *Area Group Q*

It's not about dashing around sticking plasters on things, because plasters fall off. So I mean somebody once said about chaplaincy that presence precedes proclamation. So it's done week after week, month after month, year after year sometimes. And then you might just have that one conversation that will make a phenomenal difference in that person's life. So in all our coming alongside people, we have to go the extra mile and we have to be prepared to be there, just go on doing it and then they might say "why do you do this?", "Well actually because . . . " And there's your opening to talk about things deeper. But in the meantime you are trying to enter into their pain to a certain extent and make something of it, hopefully help their pain to be transformed into something positive but it's all in a long time, it's not a quick fix, absolutely not. And it's taking their pain.

Respondent, *Area Group A*

These forms of missional witness also extended beyond chaplaincy to include a wide range of settings in which deacons found themselves, where their relationships gave rise to opportunities to model and share their faith.

3.2.5.   Encouraging and Enabling

Within these accounts of diaconal ministry, there was a recurring recognition by the deacons that their role was not just to do this diaconal ministry themselves. Indeed, underpinning the four aspects of missional presence, discernment, service and witness, deacons saw a fifth key focus of their role. This was to do what one deacon called "all the E words"—to enable, encourage and equip others to be involved within all these elements of diaconal ministry. This fifth focus was identified in all but one of the area group interviews.

Indeed, in line with the official Methodist Conference statement *What is a Deacon?*, and as noted from the outset of this book, deacons recognised that all Christians (including presbyters and lay people) are called to a life of service. Therefore, deacons did not understand the responsibility of responding to needs in churches and communities to be solely theirs. Instead, many deacons understood a critical component of their ministry to be enabling[11] and encouraging those within the Church to be involved in forms of diaconal ministry as part of the Church's wider mission. In this, they sought to bring the whole people of God into diaconal encounters with others through presence which prompts discernment, service and witness in response. One deacon described this aspect of their ministry as:

> Actually taking the needs of the world into the church community and encouraging them to address them themselves rather than thinking, "well we've got a deacon, so the deacon can do this".
>
> **Respondent, *Area Group T***

Because many deacons recognised that their practice should include enabling and encouraging the whole people of God to participate in diaconal ministry, a key indicator of good practice which surfaced in the research was when a church took a particular need on board and continued to respond to it. In fact, when speaking of successful projects, deacons would often recount instances where the work in which they had been involved had continued to flourish well beyond their own involvement.

Even one deacon who was less comfortable with "jargon words" like "enabling" and "encouraging" thought that it was crucial that the process of deacon's ministry was about "taking people with you once you've identified where the needs are". This deacon went on to describe how the deacon should allow "the church congregation, with you, to address that need so that you make yourself in a way redundant, because they then take it on board and continue it" (Respondent, *Area Group T*).

Clearly, the continuation of a particular project was not the only indicator of success, as it was not always considered appropriate for every piece of work to continue indefinitely. Indeed, deacons also spoke of instances of good practice where they were involved in helping some ministries to die gracefully, in order that others may grow in their place. Yet, to the extent that a piece of work did appropriately continue, it signified how good practice in diaconal ministry was not simply about a deacon and a deacon's own work, but was also about the connections they had formed and the way they had enabled others to participate in that ministry.

At times, as the quotations in the book have already made clear, this created particular issues for deacons, as they sometimes struggled to articulate how their own role as a deacon could be distinguished from those others, lay or ordained, who became involved in these broader aspects of diaconal ministry. These issues are explored further in Chapter 6. Nevertheless, the inter-related missional aspects of presence, service, discernment, witness and enabling others to become involved were clearly central to their understandings of what their ministry involved.

3.2.6.   A Ripple Effect

This raised particular questions about how these different key aspects of a deacon's ministry might be understood as relating to each other. In seeking to explore these questions, we looked again at the accounts of particular instances of good practice given by the deacons, and in particular how one thing led to another. What was striking was how often the deacon's initial contribution was something relatively small, and yet it led (often unexpectedly) to potentially transformative encounters. In turn, these encounters often developed a momentum of their own, in which the initial grace shown by the deacon led to a ripple effect of widening consequences as grace spread and grew, through which deacons saw God moving through his Spirit.[12] Within this ripple effect, with no expectations on those with whom they engaged, deacons nevertheless frequently found an emergent potential for significant change. **This potential arose out of the theologically reflective engagement of the deacon in the situation, in which they found ways to combine aspects of presence, service, discernment, witness and enabling others.**

Within this, the deacons typically saw their own initial contribution as something very small, but which nevertheless created a space or opportunity for this ripple effect to start. For example, many deacons spoke of doing simple acts of service, or of spending time talking to people in a particular context, without any conditions attached. Often, they preceded their description of their particular contribution with the word "just".[13] This seemed to intentionally minimise their own contribution to the process and to highlight their lack of expectation that anything would necessarily occur as a result. For example, deacons in various area groups described the importance of "just being there" in a range of difficult situations, such as when family members are ill or disabled, often "just listening", "just recognise someone's needs by their body language", "just helping them out", "just holding them while they cry". One deacon described how she had "just picked up a hoe and helped [one woman] in the garden in the prison". These simple acts could carry profound potential for transformation. For example, following one such opportunity, a deacon described how:

> I went back later and sat and just took the woman's hand; she was beyond conversation, but that didn't matter, but it just matters how we approach people and how we let people approach us, doesn't it? And give them space to open their hearts and be healed, because that's another part of ministry that is important to me.
>
> **Respondent,** *Area Group Q*

Two good examples of the way that God's Spirit was seen to gradually work through such simple things within the opportunities created by diaconal ministry were described in the following accounts:

> From those [small] actions [of service] comes a lot of wonderful things . . . I would instinctively pick up a broom and go and sweep the front of [the building to clear] all the cigarette stubs. And one particular morning there was a girl who was alcohol-dependent who was in tears and she came up to me and said . . . "I need to talk, I need to talk". Within minutes, we were making her a cup of coffee, sitting her down, relaxing her, and on that same day she went out to a clinic which would help her stop drinking alcohol. So it's from doing those little things like going out and sweeping the front that creates such a beautiful thing throughout and makes your day, makes your week. It's those precious things.
>
> **Respondent,** *Area Group U*

And sometimes it's doing just the next thing that you see, you know like this mothers' and toddlers' group. I just saw one or two mums pushing pushchairs around [the estate] and I knew there was nowhere for them to meet so I invited them in for coffee and it built up. I mean it started off with five young mums and their little ones and I think the most I had was 28 little ones and 21 mums. Fortunately it was a nice big lounge! . . . And it was lovely to see them linking up, making friends because they'd moved onto this housing estate, went out to work all day and suddenly they are left at home with a little one and don't know anybody. So it was just wonderful and to hear them say "I'll babysit for you that night, can you do it for me another night?" . . . And there was one girl came to me when I was in the kitchen at one point and she came and said ". . . I just want to thank you for doing this." And I said "oh it's great, it's lovely that you can come." "No" she said, "you've saved my life." And I thought well . . . she'd had terrible post-natal depression and didn't know what to do with herself and she came along and found friends. You know it's just doing that next thing and allowing God to unroll it as it were and develop it which I found very exciting.

Respondent, *Area Group Q*

The way this patient approach worked was described clearly in another example, given by a deacon who had just sought to meet people on first arriving in an area:

When I first came to [this city], I was told that the sheltered housing unit had a coffee morning to which anybody in the village was welcome to go. So I thought I'd be polite and you had to get somebody to let you in because it had got [locked] doors, so I went and saw the warden and said "I'm the new deacon in the area and I've been told I can come in to coffee, is that alright?" She said, "Oh no, we don't allow clergy in here". And I said "Oh, I'm sorry, I was misinformed. I don't want to push in where I'm not wanted." So she said "Oh well, if some of the residents want you, then they can invite you in to their own flat, but you can't come into the communal areas at all." So I said "Ok". And there was one member of the church who lived in the flats at that time and so of course I started visiting her. And then another Methodist moved in, so I started visiting her.

And then some of the other residents were jealous because they knew that those two were being visited regularly and they wanted somebody from the church to visit them. So . . . at one of their communal meetings they got together and they asked the Warden if I would be allowed to go to coffee mornings and to go to some of these other people as well. And they took a vote on it and the vote said "yes I could".

So I started going to their coffee mornings once a week, and that continued on for another year and the Warden got to know me a bit and started unloading some of her personal problems onto me and used me quite a lot. And then again at one of their meetings there was a group of residents that asked if they could have a service in the lounge and again the vote said "yes", and so I was invited to take a short half hour service once a month . . . and there is now twelve or fifteen people going to that service. And also . . . the Warden at that particular place had changed and the new Warden had been talking to the Warden of another sheltered housing unit down the road and saying how good these services were and some of her people were asking her for services so they invited me to start a service there as well. And that's still going as well . . . but to me it illustrates the fact that you don't always see things straight away and you often just have to work quietly underneath everything before you see any results, and you may not see any results at all.

Respondent, *Area Group T*

In accounts like this, deacons described a long process that required a difficult balance of not pushing connections prematurely, letting them develop in their own time, whilst at the same time being alert to, discerning and responding to opportunities at key moments. These moments usually occurred at the invitation of those concerned. In response to this invitation, relationships could then be developed further, new links formed, faith shared, or even a fresh expression of church developed in that context.

KEY QUESTIONS

1. How should presence, service, discernment, witness and enabling others relate together within the life and mission of the Church?
2. Is the Church's presence and service always unconditional, or are there conditions attached?
3. What forms of presence and types of engagement best reflect the Gospel?
4. How might the Church create more opportunities through which 'ripples of grace' might start, arising from the presence and service of Christians in local communities?

3.3.   CHAPTER 3 CONCLUSION

Through the forms of missional presence, service, discernment and witness they modelled, deacons described ways of making a wide range of connections between diverse people. By connecting these aspects of their practice together, they brought the Gospel to life in creative ways that formed and built new relationships between them within the diverse settings in which they operated. Whilst their ministries appeared to vary considerably between these settings, there were underlying processes within their ministries that were shared. These underlying processes often involved enabling others to get involved alongside them, and offering unconditional presence and service which created opportunities for building relationships. From these relationships, they often encountered a ripple effect of change, as they saw God's Spirit move in grace-filled ways.

Deacons saw themselves as adapting their implicit understanding of these processes to the different needs of the different Circuits in which they were stationed. Nevertheless, there were also common tensions and dilemmas within their ministries, not least in communicating the underlying nature of this diverse work to others. There is potentially much to be learned by engaging in further theological reflection on the issues that arose as a result of the ways that deacons connected the different elements of their work. As the examples in this chapter have illustrated, and the next chapter will go on to explore further, making these connections can also help the Church to make connections between the diverse people who are involved in these processes. Deacons' experiences provide a particularly rich source of experience of the opportunities and challenges involved in making these connections, which could offer much to the Church as she reflects on her involvement in God's mission in the contemporary context.

NOTES

1. Methodist Church in Britain 2004.
2. Methodist Church in Britain 2004, p. 3.
3. To reflect this distinction, this book uses "deacon's ministry" to refer to the ministry of those ordained as deacons, as distinct from the broader "diaconal ministry" which is also done by others.
4. The particular role played by deacons' identities in their diaconal ministry is explored in Chapter 5, and the relationship between different ministries and what might distinguish between them, is explored further in Chapter 6.
5. Various theologians have contributed towards a renewed interest in the missional church in ways that are relevant here; see, for example, Bosch 1991; Guder 1998; Newbigin 1995; Van Gelder 2007. Voices such as these have called for a reappraisal of ecclesiology that seeks to diminish the distinctions between *church* and *mission*. The contributors to this conversation are urging the church to conceive of itself principally as being sent by God into the world to participate in God's mission. Aspects of the missional church literature which resonate particularly strongly with parts of the research findings include the following: (1) That the Church doesn't have a mission, but rather that the Church is a mission; (2) that the Church has been sent into the world to participate in God's mission; and (3) that being missional involves looking for where God is working redemptively in the world and participating in that. In this context, the whole life of the Church and the ministries of everyone belonging to it should be missional; see Avis 2005. This clearly includes the ministry of deacons, with deacons as ordained ministers focusing this purpose in a particular way through their own contribution alongside other ministries.
6. Methodist Diaconal Order 2010.

7. These themes are picked up again later in this chapter, particularly in Sections 3.2.4 and 3.2.6.

8. This understanding has been reflected across a broad range of denominations, albeit in different forms; e.g. see Barnett 1981. In a Methodist context, for instance, see the 2004 statement of the Methodist Church in Britain *What is a Deacon?* (Section 3.3), which states that the task of the deacon is to focus the service ministry of the church. As recognised in the introduction to this book, some recent scholarship (e.g. by Collins 1990, 2002) has sought to broaden this understanding, particularly in terms of including further connotations of "commissioned agency", "ambassador" or "go-between". This scholarship has drawn on Biblical and early church uses of the Greek word "diakonia" and its cognates, from which the word "deacon" ultimately developed. See Gooder 2006, 2008 for a summary of the continuing debates around this.

9. This reflected Section 5.2 in *What is a Deacon?* which states: "The core emphasis of the ministry of deacons can therefore be characterised as witness through service. This is expressed in embodied acts of pastoral care, mercy and justice, and being or acting as a prophetic sign".

10. These dynamics of service were further complicated by their interaction with the history of the Order, as Sections 6.3.3 and 6.3.4 explore.

11. This also relates to the understanding in the Methodist Church in Britain 2004 paper *What is a Deacon?* which states in Section 3.3 that enabling others is "the primary purpose" of a deacon's ministry.

12. Morisy 2004 pp. 32–33 describes a similar process in her book "Journeying Out: A New Approach to Christian Mission", which she calls a "cascade of grace". A number of deacons referred to this book during the course of the research, and Morisy was invited to Convocation during the research period.

13. This theme occurred at least 35 times in 12 different area groups.

4. MAKING CONNECTIONS: A KEY PURPOSE OF A DEACON'S MINISTRY

4.1. INTRODUCTION TO CHAPTER 4

The way that deacons made connections between presence, service, discernment, witness and enabling others was not the only way in which "making connections" emerged as a central theme in the research. Indeed, deacons also frequently described themselves as making connections between the diverse individuals and groups of people whom they encountered in their ministry. This theme was common within the words, phrases and metaphors used by deacons to describe the particular focus of their ministry. These words and phrases included "linking", "making connections", "being a conduit", "networking", and "building bridges". This understanding of a deacon's role as "making connections" appeared in 20 out of the 22 area group interviews. Importantly, the theme of "making connections" began to develop in the analysis as an accurate way of representing the particular *aims and intentions* of a deacon's ministry. Thus, forming connections emerged as a clear answer to the question of what deacons' ministry *seeks to do*, reflecting a central component of the processes and narratives of good practice described.

Deacons saw their role in forming connections as having multiple dimensions. Some of these related mainly to building relationships within churches, others related mainly to building relationships within wider communities, and still others related to building the links between them. In addition, deacons frequently saw their ministry as helping to make connections between people across these settings and God.

Within this, deacons typically saw themselves as operating across a wide range of different contexts and settings, whilst often simultaneously being on the "edge" of them all. Because deacons' ministries often existed at the thresholds between various different communities, deacons found themselves simultaneously belonging to multiple communities. Because of this multiple belonging, they were able to act as conduits linking different groups of people together. This position also meant that they were frequently in the position of representing one group to another, as a means of building connections between groups that otherwise might not interact. This position of being on the edge of various different communities also meant that they could also take a role in linking those who felt marginalised by particular communities back into feeling more included in these communities (whether these communities were in the church, or were located in wider society).

4.2.   BRIDGING BETWEEN CHURCHES
AND WIDER COMMUNITIES

The first way in which deacons saw themselves as being present in multiple communities and trying to build connections between them was in a bridging role between churches and wider communities.

In building these connections, deacons saw it as crucial that they belonged in both churches and places in wider society that had no links with them. For example, one deacon summed up her ministry by saying, "it was all about one foot in the world and one foot in the church" (Respondent, *Area Group N*). Another stated how "deacons have been described as having a foot on the pavement and a foot in the porch and really that's what it's about" (Respondent, *Area Group A*).

While images of deacons being in the porch or being a bridge were often mentioned, some deacons also critiqued these analogies for being too static. In particular, these images did not quite capture the dynamic sense of how deacons saw themselves as belonging in different places simultaneously and moving between them. Nor did they quite capture the relational aspect of *how* they saw their contributions to these different places as being connected. For example, one deacon developed the feet analogy further to try to show how the deacon's role in different locations was different, but linked:

> My interpretation of being a deacon is, one foot inside the Church pastorally caring for, encouraging, enabling, empowering spiritual growth, that's through teaching and bringing up the gifts so the people can keep on doing. The other foot within the community sharing the love of God and bringing the needs of the community to the people of the Church.
>
> **Respondent, *Area Group P***

Many deacons further recognised that there were difficulties with over-simplified models that polarised "Church" and "world", because churches were clearly operating *within* a wider society. Deacons often sought to find language to express a much more dynamic and fluid relationship which involved the deacon positioning themselves within a web of multiple and diverse sets of relationships, and then moving between them. One deacon described the importance of the deacon's position between these diverse sets of relationships in the following way:

> I think part of it is about positioning. You know we talk about being on the edge, don't we? And I think for me there is a sense that you are on the edge of Church, if you like. You know this looking into and commenting on and representing the world and justice issues and so on and bringing them in [to the Church]. But also [the deacon is involved in] looking out at the world from a Church perspective and sharing faith. And there is lots of commenting that needs to go on at the moment about where the Church is and how we do that, you know the gap that has arisen between Church and society and there are huge issues. And I think the deacon being placed where he or she is on that edge enables . . . (there are so many images for deacons) [but] it's the bridge, the building of connections.
>
> **Respondent, *Area Group G***

As this quotation shows, by consciously positioning themselves "on the edge" of particular churches, at times deacons found themselves in situations where they represented these churches to those around them in the wider society. One deacon described this as "people on the edge receiving the best of the Church rather than the worst" (Respondent, *Area Group S*).

Deacons emphasised the importance of bringing churches into wider communities, and particularly saw their role as promoting the formation of meaningful links with those who have no other connections with churches, and showing them that churches cared about them.

> I never hide who I am and what I'm about but I don't ever push it down people's throats . . . but I actually care about them. It's giving them love. One of the things I did in my last appointment was I was chatting to the ambulance station [crew] and I used to go once a week. Very often you'd go in and there were no crews there, [because] they were out. So I always washed up for them. So I went, because you never knew when they'd come back, but they always knew I'd been because all the cups were clean. And they knew I was there on behalf of the Church, because you don't go in [specifically] as a Methodist. So it was about giving them a good experience that the Church cared, God cared, about who they were and the job they did, and they did some pretty awful jobs . . . That was my intent; it wasn't always with words but with actions that I cared about them.
>
> **Respondent, *Area Group U***

This also involved representing not just the Church but also God to these groups, with deacons using phrases like, "being Christ". One deacon described this aspect of the bridging nature of their practice as:

> Building up those networks with people in the community who may not have much faith and sort of enabling them to encounter God in the conversations that you have and representing God really as a deacon and a member of the Church.
>
> **Respondent, *Area Group G***

Some deacons went on to stress the importance of developing these links further, to invite individuals to attend church services. For example:

> This is something we've got to think about, because whatever we may say about it, our numbers aren't so great and we do need people in. We do have one or two young mums coming in to services and it's really wonderful that they are bringing their children during

the church and it's a Tuesday club. It's very lovely that this can be happening. People do like to see that there is some response.

Respondent, *Area Group T*

However, other deacons strongly resisted sentiments such as this, believing that the number of people brought into any particular church as a result of their ministry was not the best means of understanding or evaluating the effectiveness of their bridging practice. Indeed, as one interviewee contended:

It's a learning curve for the church to accept and acknowledge that just because you are doing something for the community doesn't mean to say that you are going to get all these parents and children into your church.

Respondent, *Area Group R*

After acknowledging the difficulties these expectations created, she continued:

The church still looks at this nursery school and says, "well, why aren't they coming to our church?" And you have to keep on reinforcing that a lot of these children go to other churches and some of them don't want to go to church.

Sometimes, deacons saw their work as ministry that was about helping people to heal holistically, regardless of whether they ever decided to come to church or to a Christian faith. For example, one deacon described ministering to a "loan shark" on a particular housing estate, who had no interest in becoming a Christian:

This isn't about agenda . . . I wasn't trying to ease her in church on Sunday morning, but [it was] about helping her become a whole human being really. And that's where I think the church has struggled sometimes, when [church members expect that] what you do has to translate not only into bums on seats but the "right-shaped" bums on the seats. And that's the difficult bit.

Respondent, *Area Group Q*

These quotations illustrate how deacons were often reluctant to consider their ministry entirely in terms of bringing people into particular existing churches. However, the analysis did uncover how one underlying purpose of their practice was to clear a path, so that those who so wished could start making their way towards God and the wider Church. One deacon described this as creating "a soft bridge":

> Some of those people I found who said "I don't do Church", [to whom] I say "That's fine; I'm not here to talk Church." And I think that for me is diaconal ministry, that is at the heart of my diaconal ministry, is actually meeting people who are outside of the Church who sometimes actually feel completely . . . not against the Church, but disenfranchised, they don't feel that the Church has anything to offer them. A lot of people get hurt by the Church. And I see sometimes what deacons do is create a soft bridge, the beginnings . . . the footings of a bridge for a person to start making their way back towards or to Church where they have never ever been. And that for me is strongly diaconal ministry.
>
> **Respondent, *Area Group R***

As this quotation shows, sometimes deacons saw this as a preparatory work, rebuilding and healing people's potential for relationships with God and churches, especially where their potential for building these relationships may have been previously damaged.

By being present and offering unconditional service, deacons did not see their ministry as being about seeking some form of spiritual reciprocation for this service, or somehow coercing people to faith. Instead, it was about holistically ministering to needs and meeting people where they were. Nevertheless, deacons did see themselves as representing God and the Church, and so sought ethical ways of building potential bridges and connections through their presence, discernment, service, and witness. Their understandings of holistic ministry meant that this response to needs was not restricted to purely secularised social work. Instead, it necessarily had to include introducing the Christian faith, at the times and places in which this explanation of their faith was considered ethically appropriate. This introduction of the Christian faith was often determined to be particularly ethical when it was offered in response to the requests of those with whom they were ministering. For example, one deacon described their involvement with a day centre working with people who drank alcohol on the streets, and had been asked to take a memorial service following the death of an attendee:

> And for me . . . the work I'd been doing getting alongside both the drinkers and the staff over the years has been absolutely wonderful . . . Maybe some people would class it as social work, but then to be asked to do this memorial service and then subsequently other memorial services was wonderful to link both the spiritual and the very practical work of diaconal ministry.
>
> **Respondent,** *Area Group T*

Importantly, this ambassadorial role was not merely a one-way representation, where deacons simply represented the Church in wider contexts. It was instead seen as a two way process, in which deacons also brought issues and concerns from others in wider society to the attention of those within churches. For instance, one interviewee spoke of the importance of her ordination promises to "[hold] before God's people the needs of the world" (Respondent, *Area Group A*). She described how bringing the stories of sex workers back to a largely middle-class church community had "enabled this community to see things differently". Subsequently, those within this church had been able to build relationships with this group of women, as a result of "the girls [now] being known to them".

At times, this conveying of the voices of those outside the Church could be an awkward role for deacons, especially where they had to say some unpalatable things to particular gathered congregations who were not open to hearing those voices. In fact, several deacons interviewed spoke of their role as being agitators within churches when making these representations, with one particular deacon saying, "as deacons, I was told that we are the irritant of the Church; we are that little bit of grit that the pearl grows round and our job is to irritate the Church" (Respondent, *Area Group T*).[1] While this particular interviewee went on to say that it was important to "irritate in a loving way, not irritate in an unpleasant way", it was clear that deacons did bring challenges and questions to the Church in the form of the outsider's voice. This challenge to the *status quo* had the potential to place them in uneasy positions *vis-à-vis* Church leaders and members.

However, out of this unsettling nature, the relationships built by deacons often meant that opportunities were created to develop "Fresh Expressions of Church" reaching new groups of people.[2] In developing worship that was relevant and accessible to these new groups of people, these "Fresh Expressions of Church" did not necessarily follow the traditional patterns or times of worship of existing congregations. For example, one deacon spoke of worship that had developed out of a parent and toddler group linked to a local nursery school. This deacon went on to describe the difficulties of trying to connect members of the existing Sunday morning congregation with this worshipping community:

> We do once a month toddler praise where the nursery school and the Friday morning toddler and tots group comes into the church and we have a bit of fun and we have a story and a sing song and that's church . . . We *are* involved in the Church—but it's not Sunday! And of course when you say to the . . . elderly folk who may be making one or two twitchy comments about it, you say "well, why don't you come on that Friday in the month?" [and you get the response] "Oh, well, I'm very busy you know!"
>
> **Respondent, *Area Group R***

In other settings, deacons had succeeded in making links between these emerging forms of church and traditional ventures. For example, one deacon described developing a "messy church"[3] which had involved using a range of arts and crafts activities with children and their families:

> I think it's the very early stages, but the messy church in one of the village churches [shows this link] . . . I went into the toddler group and also encouraged other people in the church to come into the toddler group—which is sort of just run by the mums. We're just in there building the relationships and the links. Some of the other people from the church—two other couples—came in and made drinks and things and just got to chatting with the mums. And then when we started messy church, they were sort of on board because we've got the relationships there already. And it has spread by word of mouth from that group really. One mum sort of takes some posters into school, another one makes some playdough every week, so they sort of got a bit of ownership of the messy church. I

think there's lots of things not right with messy church, but I think that is one thing that has sort of been good as we've started it really.

Respondent, *Area Group K*

In developing such "Fresh Expressions of Church", deacons frequently faced issues with traditional congregations about whether these expressions were recognised as "real" churches. This could potentially lead to dilemmas about what to do in particular circumstances when these communities wanted to develop other marks of being a church in their own emerging acts of worship. For example, one deacon described a situation where a messy church had developed to the point that there were requests for baptism within that environment:

Yeah, so it seems like one of the issues that I've had to face . . . is that what happens when of these families says to us they want their child to be baptised at messy church? So there's a bit of theology thrown in at the deep end. Because you have to point out to [the wider church congregation], if you've got members of the church there who are actually helping to run it, it is actually as effective as a [part of the] church [in its own right].

Respondent, *Area Group K*

Such issues are increasingly being recognised and debated within the developing literature on Fresh Expressions of Church for all those involved in establishing them.[4] Deacons recognised these issues as being vitally important; for example, one deacon claimed:

The Church has got to rediscover what it's all about. It's lost its mission in a way . . . we've tried to grasp the fact that we've got do something about our situation ourselves, [and therefore the challenge is now] learning or rediscovering what it is to be a Church again.

Respondent, *Area Group P*

Deacons in this research saw themselves as making a particular contribution to their development where these emerging forms of Church developed out of the relationships they had formed as deacons with diverse communities that had little other connection with established churches.

4.3.   FORMING CONNECTIONS WITHIN CHURCHES

Because of deacons' sensitivity to the margins, they also often found themselves making connections and forming links with those who, although they were a part of a church, nevertheless remained disconnected or isolated in some ways from it. One deacon explained it in this way:

> When I said those on the margins in society, I would certainly also want to underline that every church I've ever been there are those on the margins of any church and within the church, and they are not always the same people. In one church it might be young people, another church it might be the old people, in other churches it might [be another group] . . . but somewhere or other . . . it's [ministering to] those on those margins.
>
> **Respondent, *Area Group H***

In these instances, deacons were often able to provide a vital connection for those within the church who "have been forgotten by the church" (Respondent, *Area Group L*). This deacon shared that her ministry had included going to those who have "not been to church for years because they can't go and there has been a gap, because they just slid off the end . . . As deacons we tend to pick up the people who slide off the end, if you like."

As this deacon and several others mentioned, this included visiting those who had become housebound due to age or disability, for whom they sought means of inclusion within the church community. For example, they would often take extended communion out to these people, as a symbolic way of including them within the church's life and worship. Another example was the way that deacons sometimes developed luncheon clubs or other initiatives where people could be picked up from their homes and given opportunities to lessen their sense of isolation. It was not necessarily deacons who always undertook these tasks, and nor did deacons think it should be. However, many deacons felt that they had a particular responsibility to contribute to identifying individuals and groups who were excluded where their needs had not been previously recognised. In addition, they spoke frequently of drawing others' attentions to these needs so that there could be a wider response which they could then facilitate. For example, one deacon described how she had developed a system for ensuring that ministry teams engaged in regular pastoral visiting, so that particular members were not missed out. Deacons were also often involved in working alongside other ministerial colleagues to visit those who were sick or in hospital.

In addition, some deacons mentioned how, through their involvement in different parts of a particular church or Circuit's life, they could form connections between the often diverse and separate groups of people involved. For example, one deacon described how they had deliberately attended the various mid-week activities and different services in which a particular church was involved. This deacon had thus been able to create opportunities for the different people involved to meet each other, rather than just using the same building at different times of the week. Other deacons described how, by working across boundaries between churches and spotting those isolated in particular churches, deacons could draw these people together in ways that helped them and the churches to grow:

> I'm involved in four churches but seeing the overall picture of younger people, (when I say young I'm talking about maybe in their thirties), they are perhaps working isolated in their own churches. They are very committed to their own churches, but find that they are not always able to use their gifts or their skills and are put down . . . [As a deacon, I've been involved in] bringing them together, networking people, then giving them the opportunity to see that there are other likeminded [people] and others in their age group within our section of the Circuit anyway. And seeing them just blossom and grow with their gifts and coming together for fellowship; not to get them to leave their churches, but to encourage them in fellowship with one another, and then gifts have started to come out . . . It's just seeing them blossom and having the time to see the bigger picture and networking and pulling them together and getting them to meet.
>
> **Respondent,** *Area Group M*

This included examples where deacons were working on particular housing estates, including estates where there was no church building in that particular area, helping to develop a Christian response to needs in that place:

> I found my role listening to the Christians who are already living there and what they have already perceived God doing in that area. But because they've not been linked up, because they are from different denominations, [it's been] my role joining up the different Christians from different places so they can hear each other's ideas of what God is doing in that community . . . Some of those visions have been very similar and have overlapped considerably so I've been in a place where I can kind of draw that together, so together we can discern the whole vision for that community as it continues to grow.
>
> **Respondent,** *Area Group J*

Hence, in building these connections, deacons could stimulate forms of mission and service by bringing others together in a process of collective discernment and action, and by coming alongside them and encouraging them in this process.

4.4.   FORMING CONNECTIONS WITHIN WIDER COMMUNITIES

Similarly, deacons also articulated how their ministry was about establishing connections with those on the "margins of society" who experienced isolation and disconnectedness from the wider community:

> It's been about the Church working with those on the margins of society . . . giving a bit of affirmation and support to individuals who perhaps . . . are the most vulnerable we've got.
>
> **Respondent,** *Area Group H*

Another deacon saw their work as being "very diaconal because it is seeking the people who are forgotten about".

Beyond simply making interpersonal connections with those resting on the margins, deacons also spoke about the importance of forming dynamic organisational links within the wider communities. Deacons described good practice examples where they were involved in setting up multi-agency forums that enabled people to respond better to needs involving other statutory agencies and voluntary groups. For instance, one deacon described how they had pulled together a group of agencies who had all encountered those who were victims of trafficking, helping these agencies to talk to each other about their experiences and develop improved collective responses. Another described how she was the only person who linked a particular group of churches and agencies together. This had subsequently proved essential to establishing a new "Street Pastors"[5] initiative in an effective way, due to the multi-agency support that was mobilised through this deacon's existing relationships. In these instances, deacons served as a community hub, becoming a catalyst for forming connections between various state agencies, community workers, and charities as a result of their multiple relationships with them.

KEY QUESTIONS

1. How might the dynamic relationship between churches and wider communities be better understood beyond over-simplified models that polarise "church" and "world"?

2. How can churches be supported to create stronger links and improved learning between the different groups and individuals involved in them?

3. Is there anything distinctly "Christian" about a deacon's activity in forming connections within wider communities? If so, what? If not, should there be?

4. (a) What contributions might a deacon's ministry make to the ongoing conversation concerning the development of "Fresh Expressions of Church"? (b) What are the specific issues of which deacons should be mindful when exploring "Fresh Expressions of Church" in their ministries? (c) How can more links, greater understanding and mutual learning be encouraged between emerging and more traditional forms of Church?

4.5.   **CHAPTER 4 CONCLUSION**

This chapter has explored how deacons form a wide range of connections within their ministry between diverse individuals and groups, both within and outside existing church membership. Within this, deacons have often understood their role as including being a representative of the Church to those in need—especially those marginalised by society and the Church. Deacons also saw themselves as representing the voices of the "outsider", speaking prophetically in wider society and conveying these voices back into the heart of the Church. In the process, they have tried to create spaces and opportunities for relationships to be developed. By doing this themselves, deacons also emphasised the importance of showing how others can do this too, whilst also helping to encourage those developing such initiatives and connecting together those already involved. In this wide range of ways, deacons recognised that their contributions of presence, service, discernment, witness and enabling others could help form and strengthen connections between diverse individuals and groups, within and between churches and wider communities.

NOTES

1. Interestingly, research with community development workers turns up similar analogies—see Banks et al. 2007.

2. According to Cray 2013, the phrase "Fresh Expressions of Church" "is a way of describing the planting of new congregations or churches which are different in ethos and style from the church which planted them; because they are designed to reach a different group of people than those already attending the original church. There is no single model to copy but a wide variety of approaches for a wide variety of contexts and constituencies. The emphasis is on planting something which is appropriate to its context, rather than cloning something which works elsewhere"; see http://www.freshexpressions.org.uk/about/introduction. For further discussions of "Fresh Expressions of Church", see, for example, Croft 2008; Nelstrop et al. 2008.

3. "Messy Church" as described by a founding organisation (see Bible Reading Fellowship 2013) "is a way of being church for families involving fun; is a church, not a craft club, that helps people encounter Jesus as Lord and Saviour; is found

across the world; values are about being Christ-centred, for all ages, based on creativity, hospitality and celebration." See http://www.messychurch.org.uk.

4. Again, see, for example, the discussions in Croft 2008; Nelstrop et al. 2008.

5. Street Pastors is described by its founding organisation (Ascension Trust 2013a) as "an inter-denominational Church response to urban problems, engaging with people on the streets to care, listen and dialogue . . . There are now some 9,000 trained volunteers in around 250 teams around the United Kingdom. Each city project is set up by Ascension Trust and run by a local coordinator with support from Ascension Trust and local churches and community groups, in partnership with Police, Council and other statutory agencies." (see http://www.streetpastors.co.uk/) The role is described in the following way by the Ascension Trust (2013b): "A Street Pastor is a Church leader/minister or member with a concern for society—in particular young people who feel themselves to be excluded and marginalised—and who is willing to engage people where they are, in terms of their thinking (i.e. their perspective of life) and location (i.e. where they hang out—be it on the streets, in the pubs and clubs or at parties etc.) . . . As the Street Pastor gets to know people in the community he/she will find out their needs are and what can be done to help. A presence of Street Pastors will earn credibility in the community, so that people know that the Church is there for them in a practical way . . . Each Street Pastor team consists of at least three groups of four, each of which will work a minimum of one night a month, usually from 10pm to around 4am." (see http://www.streetpastors.co.uk/WhatisaStreetPastor/tabid/96/Default.aspx)

5.   THE ROLE OF DEACONS IN MODELLING DIACONAL MINISTRY

5.1.   INTRODUCTION TO CHAPTER 5

The book so far has outlined a range of elements of diaconal ministry and a range of people with whom deacons work, with deacons describing their ability to connect these two as a key part of their ministry. However, to understand deacons' contributions, it is essential to see them as just that: one contribution to a much wider picture. In this wider picture, deacons sought to model a diaconal ministry which was part of the mission of the whole Church, in which others could get involved. Indeed, deacons themselves saw a crucial part of their ministry as enabling others to engage within this wider diaconal ministry. Hence, it is also crucial to reflect further on how this work related to the deacons' own identities, as well as the contributions of others within wider communities and the wider Church. It is to these debates that this chapter and Chapter 6 will now turn.

5.2.   A DEACON'S IDENTITY IN FORMING CONNECTIONS

As outlined in the introduction to this book, the analysis of good practice developed through this research sees a deacon's ministry as something that connects and integrates a whole range of factors. These factors include the processes and purposes that have been explored in Chapters 3 and 4, which deacons seek to connect through their ministry. Nevertheless, in exploring deacons' examples, it has already begun to become apparent that *who the deacon is* plays a central role within *how they are able to connect* the different people and dimensions within their ministry. Indeed, a key theme of the research findings was that it is important to understand the way that *who deacons are* and *what deacons offer* contribute to their ministry. Many deacons saw their own identity and character as crucial in enabling them to make new connections when bringing the various dimensions of their ministry together. This section will explore this theme as an introduction to the wider issues, tackled subsequently in Chapter 6, surrounding the ways in which deacons saw their own identities in relation to the ministries of others. The role of their own identity was something which deacons often found difficult to articulate coherently. Nevertheless, it was clearly important to them and to their effectiveness in ministry.

5.2.1.   The Relationship between "Being" and "Doing" in a Deacon's Ministry

When describing the examples of good practice outlined in Chapters 3 and 4, deacons repeatedly emphasised that *who they were* was at least as important as *what they did*:

> What is it that God's calling us to be and do? I mean there are two aspects to it, but the being is so important as well.
>
> **Respondent,** *Area Group G*

> It is different to function. It's something about being; it's about who we are.
>
> **Respondent,** *Area Group N*

Indeed, many deacons saw it as much more important to focus on *being* rather than *doing*:

> I think one of the emphases of diaconal ministry is about being rather than doing.
>
> **Respondent,** *Area Group U*

> What is identifiable about being a deacon is that you move away from not "a deacon is what you do", but "it's who you are". It doesn't really matter what we do.
>
> **Respondent,** *Area Group J*

As this second quotation illustrates, some deacons emphasised *being* to such an extent that what they actually did was immaterial as long as they were being a deacon whilst doing it. When not accompanied by any deeper explanations, such perspectives sometimes contributed to a perceived lack of clarity regarding their purpose, and also to difficulties in explaining their role to others. In addition, these perspectives tended to define a deacon's ministry in a rather circular way; i.e. as being whatever a deacon did. Further confusion was often generated when this approach was combined with deacons' discussions about enabling others to become involved in aspects of diaconal ministry (as highlighted in Section 3.2.5).

However, other interpretations of this focus on *being* had a more positive impact. In these interpretations, deacons' own life stories, characters and identities, in all their diversity, became an integral part of their ministry. Consequently, they were able to offer a ministry of personal integrity, which was crucial in enabling them to make the connections outlined previously. Their own interests, backgrounds, senses of humour etc. all provided potential points of connection with others. By holding these different parts of their life together within their own person, they could forge new links through who they were. By integrating these with their own growing spiritual development, they also sought to support others in developing their relationship with God.

As noted above, many deacons recognised that a calling to such an integrated life of service was also the call of the whole people of God. As one deacon put it, "diaconal ministry is the call of every Christian" (Respondent, *Area Group D*).

Many deacons spoke of a calling to this way of life as something that had always been part of them:

> I feel that all my life I have been involved in diaconal ministry; that's what God has called me to and if it hadn't been through the Methodist Diaconal Order, it would have been through something else, because it's always been there. And as I meet other deacons, I kind of can see that actually they are deacons before training. And I guess the training is kind of affirming that and developing it, what is already there.
>
> **Respondent, *Area Group U***

This sentiment was shared by interviewees who stressed their call to a life of service—both to a life of serving God and to a life of serving others.

In light of the common nature of this calling, the deacon from Area Group D (quoted above), who recognised that diaconal ministry was the call of every Christian, nevertheless made a helpful distinction between:

1. this general call of all Christians to diaconal ministry; *and*
2. a deacon's particular call to "*ordained* diaconal ministry".

This deacon recognised that the latter calling included making a lifelong commitment in which they offered themselves to follow the discipline of a particular denomination for its ordained ministers. For deacons in the Methodist Church in Britain, this currently includes a calling to itinerancy and being stationed wherever the Methodist Church wishes to place them.

Many deacons within this context also emphasised that they felt called to the Methodist Diaconal Order as "a religious order", with one deacon saying:

> We are deacons, it's about being deacons. It's not a job description.
> It's a way of life for a start, in part of that religious order.
>
> **Respondent,** *Area Group M*

This belonging to a religious order included a common commitment to mutual support and availability to serve the Church in dispersed settings, whilst developing their own spiritual life and calling within this community. The particular contribution of the religious order to this calling is considered in more detail in Chapters 6 and 7.

5.2.2.   How a Deacon's Identity Helps to Make Connections

So how did deacons see the ways in which their identity as a member of this religious order interacted with their wider calling, alongside all Christians, to diaconal ministry?

As Chapter 4 concluded, deacons sought to make connections in a broad range of ways. The particular ways that they sought to do this were frequently integrated with who they were as a person and as a recognised ordained minister in the Church. Deacons frequently described how they found themselves personally being a representative of the Church to those in need—especially those marginalised by society and the Church itself. Deacons also saw themselves as being people who personally represented and conveyed the voices of the "outsider", carrying these voices within themselves to speak prophetically back into the heart of the Church. By doing these things as part of their own personal character and spiritual life, deacons also emphasised the importance of showing how others can do them too, whilst also helping to "give permission" to those developing such initiatives. Whilst doing this as part of their own identity, they were also aware of their role as a representative person within the Church, modelling a process of struggling to engage with the difficult issues facing the wider world from a Christian perspective. In turn, they could then encourage congregations to engage in forms of mission and service by coming alongside them in these tasks, and in doing so provide institutional permission and support for them. Throughout this process, deacons continually sought to be listeners, carers, enablers, and encouragers— modelling how all these aspects could facilitate the involvement of others.

The picture of good practice that begins to emerge from this is one of the deacon weaving together relationships between the diverse individuals and communities they encounter. All of the deacons' roles, processes and purposes link together through this "making connections" theme, with the link being the identity of the person recognised and commissioned by the Church which integrates them all.[1]

Thus, a helpful image of good practice in diaconal ministry may be seen as weaving together relationships between people both "inside" and "outside" traditional church settings. The purpose of this weaving is to form encounters, connections and improved relationships between God and others. This concept is represented in the diagram in Figure 1 (p. 66), which seeks to account for the various elements present in a deacon's ministry.

As this diagram indicates, there are multiple communities through which deacons weave. There is the church community, or rather communities, as often there are several communities within particular churches, and deacons are frequently involved in trying to connect some of those communities (as discussed in Section 4.3). There are also wider communities, and deacons are quite often connecting people across these communities in this wider context (as discussed in Section 4.4). Then, as deacons weave from one context to the next, they work to connect all

Figure 1: The "weaving" of relationships in diaconal ministry

these communities together, especially church communities and the wider communities of which they are a part (as discussed in Section 4.2). This often includes those on the fringes of the church communities, which is represented by the shaded area of this diagram.[2] Throughout, deacons themselves move through a cycle of being sent out and gathering in, working with and alongside others at different stages of the process.[3]

Within a deacon's varied ministry, a key element which holds these diverse contributions together is the integrity of the deacon. Indeed, much of the enormous diversity within deacons' practice can be accounted for by understanding that their roles change depending on which particular point in the weaving process they are at. For example:

1. when representing churches to those who have little contact with them, they may offer unconditional service to them arising from their presence alongside them;

2. when working with those on the fringes of existing congregations, they may be involved in symbolic and practical actions to link these people back into the wider body of the Church;
3. when working in churches, they may be representing the needs of excluded groups to congregation members.

All these roles need to be understood as part of a larger movement, linked into the wider Church as the Body of Christ.

5.2.3. Flexibly Negotiating Identity: Uniform and Beyond

A deacon's identity is a vital dimension of this work, because they often make flexible and reflexive use of this identity in forming their connections with others, and in linking different communities. There were many instances in which deacons indicated that good practice involved being aware of how they managed and presented themselves when going into a particular situation. From paying close attention to how they dressed, to carefully considering what they said when first introducing themselves, deacons sought to present themselves in ways that were adapted to the people with whom they were interacting.

Widespread debates within the Methodist Diaconal Order about the use of uniform exemplified the flexibility and fluidity of ways in which deacons presented their identity. Indeed, the wearing of uniform was recognised as a highly contentious issue within the order itself. We would argue that debates over uniform were so contentious precisely because they tapped into much deeper debates and dilemmas relating to these complex issues of managing personal and collective identity. Analysis of the data revealed how deacons' decisions about uniform were often linked to their notions of belonging and bridging, and how deacons navigated their identities in the midst of these two activities. For example, one deacon described reflecting on what to wear in particular situations in the following way:

> When you are in a role there, you are going to be doing so many different things, you just have to have all kinds of [clothes and ask] . . . what sort of deacon do I have to be in this situation? . . . While I'm going into Girls' Brigade, is there any point in me wearing a suit and a collar? Probably not! But I also have my navy blue jacket

that's hung up there at the moment, it's the one that gets slung in the back of the car. So if I go to something "youthy" at one point, I'll just wear a T-shirt, but if I need to look a bit smart, I can throw on the jacket and go and have a conversation with the leader of the Residents' Association. So I can be a different person for the different people that I am dealing with.

Respondent, *Area Group R*

Asking "what sort of deacon do I need to be in this situation?" meant that at times deacons would readily choose to identify themselves with the Church from first impressions through their choice of clothes. At other times, asking the same question would indicate awareness that certain clothes might act as a barrier to the process of initiating engagement: "for some, [clerical dress] will open doors, and for others it will be a barrier. You just don't know" (Respondent, *Area Group R*).

As a result, deacons' decisions about clerical dress were often made reflexively and in light of context. Deacons articulated a reflective awareness of what their dress symbolised, and the decision to wear a collar or a cross in particular situations was often based upon reflections about what would be most helpful for making connections within that particular situation. For example, one deacon indicated that when:

Doing chaplaincies and stuff, actually having an identifiable uniforming aspect opens doors for you as a minister, because the secular world identifies with that as well.

Respondent, *Area Group J*

The symbolic importance of wearing a uniform was reflected in one deacon's reflections on the importance of being seen to be representing the Church through her uniform in particular situations:

I end up being very clear about who I am—I'm there as a Methodist deacon . . . I know there are lots of people who don't do this but this is just what I do, so I actually find wearing a uniform really easy. I haven't had a single alcoholic or drug addict or homeless person or prostitute not be able to talk to me, throw up over me, tell me all the stuff of their life, despite wearing this. And I'm very deliberate and intentional and I don't think you have to wear the uniform but I'm very clear that I'm here on behalf of the Church. So the [people I'm working with], when they narrate their story of how they feel, they talk about the Church not me . . . They made a lovely thing about this as a church because they recognise that there are definite things that happen, that happen because the Church says "yes" to them.

Respondent, *Area Group A*

In this instance, and others like it, the choice to wear a uniform was often taken because it was seen as a positive asset to enabling the representative and bridging aspects of the deacon's role in that particular situation.

Some other deacons felt that not wearing a uniform in some situations allowed them to be more ambiguous about how they presented themselves, and that this could be helpful in approaching those for whom a more uniformed approach might be off-putting:

I don't often say, "Look this is who I am." Sometimes I do, because it depends on the situation . . . Sometimes I just go and be . . . you know it just depends on the situation as to whether it comes up straight away, or whether it comes up down the line.

Respondent, *Area Group L*

As this quotation illustrates, this attention to context required deacons to have a high degree of flexibility in presentations of their role which extended beyond what they wore, and thus deacons found themselves fluidly moving between different presentations of themselves to different groups in their practice. One particular deacon believed this fluidity and flexibility negatively impacted on a deacon's own identity, claiming that "you can't be flexible without being blurred". Yet for other deacons, the ability to negotiate their identity fluidly served them well in their diverse roles, as it was precisely this quality that enabled them to connect and negotiate different contexts and communities: "Is it the blurred lines that define who we are?" (Respondent, *Area Group N*).

In this sense, it was deacons' multiple memberships of different communities (albeit in different roles and capacities) which provided the potential for them to blur and bridge between them. At times, this could create difficult decisions about how best to present themselves in particular situations, particularly if there were tensions between their different presentations in different circumstances. This meant that deacons had to manage the presentation of their identity reflexively in different contexts in appropriate ways. At the same time, they sought to maintain the integrity of who they were within this process, allowing them over the longer term to build the connections between the different contexts, the people they engaged with, and the different aspects of their role.

5.2.4. The Risk that Being "Out on the Edge" Becomes "Out on a Limb"

As the previous sections have shown, this multiple membership of different communities and the deacon's movement between them can challenge the common tendency for any particular group to become insular, and helps to weave connections between them. It can also show ways in which those within churches (who also belong to multiple communities in the rest of their everyday lives) can connect others from the wider communities to which they belong with the life of the Church.

However, when considering the movement and momentum that takes place throughout this cycle, as deacons weave from one context to another, it is important that deacons do not remain just "on the edge" for too long. The constant risk inherent in this position is that the deacon themselves can become distanced and disenfranchised from the churches that send them. Deacons sometimes faced situations where they ended up only working out in wider communities, with little support or connection with their sending churches. For example, one deacon spoke of how this wider work meant that: "I've not found a place really within the Circuit team, I feel very much on the fringe of that and on the fringe of the Circuit" (Respondent, *Area Group J*).

Another spoke of how she had found herself isolated from local churches in one situation, and learnt from this for future appointments:

> There have been a couple of people who have come to me from other contexts who have said "I'm not actually at a church at the moment, I haven't got a community of believers that I'm worshipping with". And I suddenly thought "yes, that is something that's like a deep longing in me that I want to belong to". And I don't feel I belong to any of the Circuit churches . . . I now know that going to a new appointment . . . I will have to find a spiritual home in a church

> somewhere, even if I'm working across the Circuit, I will have to
> find a spiritual home somewhere, because I cannot not belong.
>
> **Respondent,** *Area Group J*

On the other hand, spending too much time within the structure of their churches can endanger the deacon's capacity to build relationships with members of communities outside them. Thus, a constant, consistent movement through the cycle is necessary for deacons to minister effectively in each context and to build connections between them. The "weaving" analogy referred to earlier helps provide a visual image of this, as does the related image of sewing.[4] Using this sewing analogy, the deacon could be thought of as a needle, providing a particular focus and sharp point to enable the thread to be woven through the material. If other Christians are thought of as the thread within this metaphor, then the deacon as the needle can help to provide a focused point which penetrates the boundaries of the material. Without the presence of this needle, the boundaries might otherwise prevent the thread of other Christians engaged in diaconal ministry from linking, binding and drawing the different communities involved closer together.

There are further particular dilemmas and challenges for deacons in that, given the nature of their work, much of it may not be visible to those within the churches that are sponsoring it:

> If I look back over twenty years, so much of what I've done has
> been outside of the church. And a lot of it, a lot of what we do I
> believe is hidden because a lot of what we do is very private and
> it's confidential . . . even if it's within the church. So a lot of our
> ministry has to remain private and unspoken . . . Whereas if you are
> working outside of the church, you are not as visible to those within
> the church and that can be difficult justifying your appointment
> in a sense.
>
> **Respondent,** *Area Group R*

Other deacons discussed how they needed to make a conscious effort to share what they were doing with those within local churches:

> I always think that it will be very useful if a deacon is in a church, to
> actually occasionally just stand up and give some good news about
> what they've been doing over the month.
>
> **Respondent,** *Area Group E*

> To tell people . . . I note little things and I just drop hints, because
> they have no idea in [our] Circuit what a deacon is.
>
> **Respondent,** *Area Group E*

Unless this link is consciously nurtured, the ability for deacons to get others involved in diaconal ministry and bring the needs of the wider world to the Church is undermined. The sustainability of this ministry is also undermined, especially where the lack of links back to worshipping communities means that the deacon's appointment is not renewed as a result, and especially if others have not become involved in this work whilst the deacon was present. One deacon described what they saw as a more positive way of practising in the following way:

> I think part of what deacons . . . [are] called to do is begin to do
> themselves out of a job wherever they are, as they are finding these
> new areas of working and they are starting things up. The idea is that
> actually I'm only here in the short term and somebody else is going
> to take on this leadership; I'm not here to lead this group [forever].

Referring back to the "sewing" analogy mentioned earlier, there is little point in the deacon being a metaphorical needle making holes between boundaries unless the needle is threaded, with the "thread" consisting of other Christians who have ownership and take on leadership of the connections that form over the longer term.

Furthermore, where there is a lack of an embedded role for deacons within established worshipping communities, there is a risk that the connection between deacons' outreach activities and worship can become severed. Some deacons were concerned that when this happened, as it often could, it then limited their ability to make connections. For example, one deacon hosted a workshop at Convocation to explore these issues with others. In addition, in conversations involving ecumenical partners from more than one other Christian denomination[5] observed during the research, those represented indicated that they felt that this was an area where Methodist practice might helpfully engage with and learn from other denominations' liturgical practices. In some denominations, aspects of deacons' ministries have traditionally been given symbolic recognition through particular liturgical contributions. For example, deacons in some denominations have been given roles such as leading intercessory prayers, reading the Gospel, and carrying a Paschal candle into the Easter service.[6] The remembering of deacons' work within church prayers said by others is another example.

Regardless of how this connection is actually made in practice, the linking of deacons' ministries to the wider life of the Church is clearly crucial. However, the nature of the precise role can be controversial in practice, for reasons explored in the next chapter. All these reasons underlined the importance of considering carefully the relationship between a deacon's ministry and the ministries of others. This is a key dimension of good practice within this ministry, as Chapter 6 will now explore.

KEY QUESTIONS

1. How should "being" and "doing" relate together within ministry?
2. What might the wider Church learn from the ways in which deacons simultaneously belong to multiple communities and use this multiple belonging to build relationships between these different communities?
3. (a) How might different parts of diaconal ministry be connected so that they form part of this wider movement of being sent out from and gathering people in to the Church? (b) What theological understandings of this work might support the making of these connections?
4. (a) How should the Church support those involved in diaconal ministry in order to avoid them ending up "out on a limb" when reaching out to those who are marginalised? (b) What should those involved in diaconal ministry do to contribute towards this?
5. In what appropriate ways might deacons' contributions to the life of the Church be recognised symbolically and liturgically within church services?

NOTES

1. They also reflect and bring together a wide range of different literature on the ministry of a deacon; see, for example, Renewed Diaconate Working Party of the House of Bishops 2001 p. 5: "The need at the present time may well be to find an overarching rationale that brings together the diverse roles—liturgical, pastoral, communal, administrative, catechetical and prophetic—that diakonia (diaconal ministry) has taken in the Church's life . . . Though models of diaconal ministry have been varied, the guiding thread seems to be the connecting nature of the diaconate". See also those reflected in contributions to Hall's (1992) edited collection, etc. They also reflect, but do not rely upon, the wider possible understandings of meanings of *diakonia* which include connotations of commissioned agency and being an ambassador referred to earlier; e.g. within Collins' (2002) and Gooder's (2006, 2008) work.

2. Indeed, this might helpfully be understood differently, in terms of "centred sets" of people coming to be focused on Christ, rather than discrete categories ("bounded sets") defined primarily in terms of membership of a group in which you are either considered "in" or "out"; see Hiebert 1979. See also the subsequent application of this work in the General Synod Board of Education 1996 report on young people and the Church, *Youth A Part*.

3. This is also strongly reflects ecumenical reflections in the Diakonia World Federation Executive Committee's 1998 paper, *Diaconal Reflections: How We Experience Our Diaconal Calling in Our Diversity*.

4. This particular image is the authors' rather than the deacons' analogy, but attempts to sum up the picture being painted through the various accounts.

5. This was particularly the case in informal ecumenical exchanges with Roman Catholic deacons, but also reflected in Anglican and wider ecumenical discussions.

6. See, for example, Fitzgerald 1992, on the deacon's role in Orthodox liturgy and Burham 1992, for a comparison from an Anglican perspective.

6. EXPLORING THE RELATIONSHIP BETWEEN DEACONS AND OTHER MINISTRIES: MAKING FURTHER CONNECTIONS

6.1. INTRODUCTION TO CHAPTER 6

So far, this book has outlined how deacons discussed their own ministries, and how different aspects of these ministries are related. However, for these ministries to be effective, there was a third dimension of good practice that was ever-present in the discussions within the data collected. This third dimension involved debates about different understandings of the *relationships between different ministries*. Indeed, the most prevalent factors that were seen to be crucial in either enabling or limiting deacons' abilities to form the wide range of connections that were described in Chapters 3, 4 and 5 were all linked to understandings of the relationships between different ministries.

Deacons frequently described instances where their weaving of connections had put them in a liminal position.[1] In moving between different domains to connect them, they were often perceived by others as intruding. Such conflicts were cited as occurring in examples involving some presbyters, lay Christians, and professionals in secular agencies within wider local communities. These tensions were exacerbated when deacons and others:

1. could not clearly and positively explain the connecting nature of the deacon's role; *and*
2. instead tended to define this role solely in opposition to the different "others" they encountered.

One deacon, having reflected on the problems that arose when deacons were defined by what they were not, concluded that a better way forward would be to "maybe define what we do, rather than what we don't do" (Respondent, *Area Group N*).

It is hoped that the work in the preceding chapters has already helped to contribute to this more positive definition of what a deacon's ministry entails. As these chapters have also indicated, it is important to ground understandings of all ordained ministry within the Church's wider understanding of the mission and ministry of the whole people of God.[2] However, there remain some important issues to be explored about how different roles and ministries relate. In particular, it is important to explore how some common current discourses and understandings were found to add to these tensions, and how these might helpfully be reviewed.

6.2.   RELATIONSHIPS BETWEEN DEACONS & OTHERS, ESPECIALLY LAY PEOPLE

So why were tensions between different ministries exacerbated when negative definitions of a deacon's role were used? Defining deacons by "what they didn't do" automatically separated them and their understandings of diaconal ministry from others. At the same time, deacons were aiming to develop forms of diaconal ministry for everyone, including lay Christians, presbyters, and (for at least some deacons) those currently outside the Church. This was done so that all might participate in this transformative ministry wherever God is at work in the wider world. Any strategy that relied on defining a deacon's role in terms of "what they were not" was problematic because if no distinction was made between a deacon's ministry and diaconal ministry, it automatically excluded some other group from diaconal ministry. As a result, whenever deacons identified something within their ministry as being distinctively diaconal, they frequently recognised that this was also shared by other ministries. **Indeed, what deacons described as distinctive about their own role was often precisely what they are seeking to enable and encourage in others.**

In addition, as discussed at the end of Chapter 5, where deacons were embodying how these connections can be made *only* in themselves, without also enabling others to be involved alongside them, there was a further potential danger. This lay in displacing wider involvement in diaconal ministry, especially if churches then relied on the deacon to "do their diaconal ministry for them". This was why the "enabling" theme of good practice was seen as such a crucial component in Chapter 3. On this basis, several deacons noted the need to distinguish carefully between a deacon's ministry and diaconal ministry. In one deacon's words:

> I think we need to be [clear] (well this is a personal angst I have), that diaconal ministry is the call of every Christian and is fulfilled by even those who don't name the name of Christ.[3] And when I am asked to go and speak about diaconal ministry, I say that I have come to talk about what it means to be in *ordained* diaconal ministry, and I think there is a difference.
>
> **Respondent, *Area Group D***

A critical analysis of their responses highlighted the importance of recognising the difference between the terms "diaconal" and "deacon".[4] This distinction lay in the nature of the reciprocally-recognised and life-long position, commitment, relationship and focal role that deacons have taken on within the Church through their ordination to this particular vocation. In British Methodism, this position has also become linked to membership of a religious order and, somewhat atypically in comparison with other denominations, it has also become linked to a commitment to ministerial itinerancy.[5]

As stated at the start of this book, this means that deacons can be understood as doing diaconal ministry, and indeed provide a focus for it, but this doesn't mean that *all* diaconal ministry is done by deacons. As one deacon commented:

> I think to an extent everybody, every Christian is called to diaconal ministry. It's just that some of us are set aside to focus it. But always it's about enabling everybody to exercise their own diaconal ministry . . . God has called us and set us aside to focus it, I think.
>
> **Respondent, *Area Group U***

This is crucially important in a context where, for a wide range of pressing theological and practical reasons outlined in Chapter 1, many churches in the contemporary context are exploring how they can empower and enable lay people to be more involved in a range of ways in the Christian life and mission. The deacons responding to the research recognized that they worked alongside others in Church leadership positions to enable this greater involvement of lay people to happen. However, deacons' accounts of practice from their ministry raised important issues concerning how the laity are recognised and supported when they do get involved in diaconal ministry in the desired way. A particular issue explored within the research was whether current prevalent discourses and practices concerning ordained ministry might disempower lay people who take on forms of leadership in this work that do not take the form of ordination and/or itinerant ministry.

As Chapter 5 explored, deacons integrated who they were as individuals with how they did their ministry, and understandably saw their integrity in doing this as a key aspect of good practice. However, when deacons emphasised the central contribution made by the deacon as a focus of diaconal ministry, there was an ever-present risk. This risk was that such discourses could be heard by others to mean that only deacons can do diaconal ministry effectively. After all, if a deacon's "being" is presented as such an essential component in good diaconal ministry, how can others who are not deacons engage within it effectively? One possibly helpful answer to this question lies in recognising that the integrity of the person engaging in diaconal ministry is indeed crucial to its effectiveness, whether this person is a deacon or not. In this view, deacons only symbolise this link by being a living example, showing how it can be done. However, deacons' discourses heard during the research sometimes presented it in a much more selective way than this, and other voices heard during the research had found this excluding.

These debates were also reflected in aspects of discussions such as those about dress which were previously explored in Section 5.2.3. Some deacons were particularly sensitive to the implications for others when they made particular choices, such as how they dressed in particular situations. Deacons also sometimes recognised ways in which these choices might have longer-term implications that might undermine their wider role in enabling others. For example, one deacon critiqued any insistence on a distinctive form of dress for deacons that might undermine their ability to engage others in diaconal ministry:

> [But] I want to say actually lay people can do those ministries as well. And if we are having to set ourselves [apart], dress differently in order to let the world identify you, then we are saying actually that makes it still really difficult for lay people to do it . . . I don't want to make myself so different from them that they can't do that ministry. I want to change the world's view of people doing it so they will accept anybody.
>
> **Respondent,** *Area Group J*

Of course, there are other situations where lay people might also choose to adopt a particular form of dress to identify themselves with the Church or a particular initiative, such as in the Street Pastor initiatives mentioned by a number of deacons.[6] This shows that the issue was a more symbolic one for them, about how particular deacons chose to present themselves in particular situations, and what this might mean for both the deacon and (more importantly) those with whom they were working.

6.2.1.   Issues of Representation

A related cluster of themes concerned issues of representation. In order to distinguish between lay and ordained ministries, one argument frequently deployed by both deacons and those in the wider Church was that those who are ordained *represent* the Church in a particular way. This representation was seen as happening by virtue of the committed two-way covenant relationship that exists between the ordained minister and the Church that ordains them. However, some deacons recognised that these issues of representation had wider implications and were more complex than they seemed.

When making initial connections with those who had little or no previous contact with the Church, many deacons felt there was a limit to which it was helpful to try to convey and explain their particular role within the Church:

> In my previous appointment when I went to schools and that, although they knew I was from the Church, I was just Heather.[7] The important thing was that they knew I was Heather, rather than that I was a deacon. They knew I belonged to the Church and it

was just being Heather and the kids would come up to me when I was walking down the street and they knew who I was. I'd talk to parents through that, but not for them to remember that I was a deacon, but that they knew who I was and [that] I came in and told them about Jesus!

Respondent, *Area Group P*

And the people in the community very quickly caught on to what you are trying to do, they accept that without question; they might not realise you are a deacon, but they accept the role that you have within the community.

Respondent, *Area Group L*

The important thing in situations like this was simply that the deacon was seen to be representing the Church, rather than trying to explain their particular position within it. Similarly, in representing the Church, the deacons sought to demonstrate more widely how service could be offered, and how diaconal ministry could engage others. For example, one deacon indicated that when Jesus washed His disciples' feet, he did so to demonstrate that others should do likewise; His choice to do this did not disempower others from also doing so. For this deacon, this also applied in contemporary settings: the deacon's involvement is intended to encourage others to engage in whatever contemporary form "footwashing" might take. For example, when working on a Street Pastor scheme, this could involve wiping vomit from the mouth of someone who has had too much to drink.

However, particular issues emerged concerning some of the discourse among presbyters and deacons which explained that "ordained ministers represented the Church by virtue of their ordination". For instance, the way in which these explanations were used could inadvertently diminish the significant ways that lay Christians might also represent the Church. This was particularly noticeable in deacons' ministries, given the importance they attributed to enabling other Christians to come alongside them in their ministries. In order to enable lay people to make these links between the Church and wider communities, it was fundamentally important that this role of representation was not seen as being restricted to those who were ordained. However, it also raised issues about how lay people who took on leadership roles in aspects of diaconal ministry might be more clearly recognised and supported by the Church.

These fundamental debates require further theological reflection, for which there is not sufficient space within this book. Nevertheless, it is important for the Church to consider its broad theology of ordination carefully, so that its discourses and actions support the wider lay involvement, leadership and range of ministries it is seeking to engender.

KEY QUESTIONS FOR ALL CHURCHES

- How might deacons and other ordained ministers speak of the nature of their ordained ministry in ways that do not inadvertently disempower lay people?
- Is it important that ordained ministry be more clearly promoted and widely understood as "representative but not exclusively representative"?
- Would this help those in lay offices/roles to be more recognised and empowered as representatives of the Church in a wider range of ways?

Underlying such debates, there was another set of questions, concerning the characteristics which are necessarily linked in the fundamental nature of diaconal ministry, as opposed to the historic way that expressions of this ministry have evolved in this particular denomination. The deacons interviewed generally saw it as imperative to retain their own relationship with the Connexion as both an order of ministry and a religious order. However, there was a recognition by some that they had initially felt called more to one than the other, with their appreciation of the two combined only developing over time. None of what is written in this section is intended to question the Methodist Church's current recognition of existing deacons belonging to both an Order of Ministry and a religious order, and their permanent full-time stipendiary Covenant relationship with the Connexion, as recognised by Conference in the report *What is a Deacon?* Indeed, the ability to engage in this ministry in a full time and stipendiary way was seen as a major asset of the Methodist Church's approach by those from a wide range of traditions encountered in the research. It was recognised that the commitment of these deacons to itinerancy was a key factor in enabling this to happen.

However, the authors' analysis occasionally raised questions about whether even more contributions to this essential ministry could be enabled by the Methodist Church opening out the current configuration in some way. Examples of these questions and related debates are given in the "Key Questions" box at the end of this section. Developing a collective response by the Methodist Church to such questions would necessarily involve further reflection and engagement with a wider range of theological literature. This could also take account of wider Methodist Church and ecumenical debates.

Deacons frequently raised the point that some lay people could choose to follow their "Rule of Life"[8], and indeed a few claimed that that was precisely the point—they sought to model a form of Christian ministry and spiritual life that others could also do. However, to enable lay people to follow all of the current "Rule of Life", the Order would need to allow them to join in the collective aspects of the Order's "Rule of Life" such as attending Convocation and Area Groups, or find other appropriate ways of structuring this involvement. The Warden of the Methodist Diaconal Order also recognised that the Order had received many enquiries (as yet unanswered or even resisted) from a range of others seeking some form of membership of the Order for a wide range of reasons, including when wanting to offer hospitality to deacons from other denominations or parts of the worldwide Methodist Church.

KEY QUESTIONS FOR THE METHODIST
CHURCH IN BRITAIN

- Are there people who are not able to be itinerant, and who may not be paid by the Methodist Church, who are nevertheless called to provide *leadership in local contexts* in terms of diaconal ministry? If these were recognised in some way, could these provide a further key focus for representing the Church in local contexts and engaging in diaconal ministry? How might this be similar to and different from the calling of all members of the Methodist Church?[9]
- If recognition is important for representation, then is there scope for formally recognising in some way those lay people who are called to take on leadership roles within aspects of diaconal ministry, or who otherwise provide a focus for diaconal work within local congregations? If so, should this be through including these in some way within the Methodist Diaconal Order, even if they may not be itinerant and/or paid?
- Which aspects should be definitive in deciding membership of the Methodist Diaconal Order as a religious order—and should these necessarily coincide with those that are currently definitive to ordination to an Order of Ministry? Should either or both necessarily coincide with itinerancy? Should either or both necessarily coincide with payment?
- If membership of the Methodist Diaconal Order as a religious order, with a commitment to following their "Rule of Life", is seen as a helpful way of fostering and supporting those who provide such a focus, then should this be restricted to just those who are ordained as deacons? For example, could there be a category of membership within the Methodist Diaconal Order as a religious order for others who provide this focus and leadership?[10]

6.3. PRESBYTER/DEACON RELATIONSHIPS

The important dimension of relationships between lay and ordained ministries was rather overshadowed in the research data by much more frequent reference to the relationship between ordained ministries within the Methodist Church. Indeed, when deacons tried to describe their role, they frequently tried to do so by first comparing themselves in opposition to presbyters in some way.[11] Deacons would regularly draw upon familiar clichéd expressions to position themselves vis-à-vis other ministries—such as by contrasting presbyters as being inward-facing with deacons being outward-facing in relation to the Church. However, deacons also frequently noted that such contrasts were limited and often problematic, as this section will now consider.

6.3.1. Freed up to be Available and Flexible

Deacons in the group interviews perceived themselves to have been freed up by the Church to be more available and flexible in their patterns of ministry than presbyters. For example, speaking to this issue of availability, one interviewee noted how this was, for her, the biggest difference between deacons and presbyters:

> If I were to sum it up in one word it would be "available". We are more "available" . . . We have more opportunities, however stiff and starchy the church congregations might be . . . to respond to what we see needs to be done than . . . a presbyter who has got a certain structure that he must do.
>
> **Respondent, *Area Group N***

This extra availability was seen as making different opportunities possible, particularly in terms of engaging more often with groups outside traditional churches. This availability linked with the themes and processes outlined in Chapter 3, particularly with the theme of "missional presence". An essential prerequisite for having such a presence was having been freed up by the Church to take the time to build new connections and relationships outside existing established patterns of ministry and existing locations. For example, one deacon said:

> My role has very much been in the community which I'm there to serve and enabling other Christians who are in that community to serve as well. And so as a deacon I'm freed up to do that. I'm not attached to any other church congregation or building and so on, very much free to serve the schools, the Residents' Association, anything that's going on in that community and be a part of [them] because I'm freed up time-wise to do that.
>
> **Respondent,** *Area Group J*

A number of deacons expressed considerable gratitude to the Church for freeing them up in this way, and giving them the time and space to get involved in this ministry whilst having their living expenses covered. However, this availability and flexibility to serve in a wider range of contexts also impacted more negatively on deacons' sense of their recognition within churches in comparison to presbyters. Because their own work was often on the boundaries and fringes of churches, some deacons felt that much of their ministry could go unnoticed. In contrast, one deacon commented:

> Because of the nature of presbyters, because they are the ones who stand up in front all the time, they're the ones that get the recognition
>
> **Respondent,** *Area Group P*

This added to the risks of deacons ending up feeling "out on a limb" as described earlier in Section 5.2.4. Their perceived additional flexibility also added to the issues regarding defining what was at the core of a deacon's roles given their diversity of expressions, as described in Section 2.1.

6.3.2.   Tensions in Discrete Definitions

The group interviews that started with deacons trying to define themselves in opposition to presbyters usually then went on to recognise that there were limitations to these polarised descriptions and even tensions and contradictions within them. In these discussions, deacons often drew on official definitions of the differences between the roles, as laid out in the Methodist Conference-approved papers *What is a Deacon?*[12] and *What is a Presbyter?*[13]. For example, one deacon said:

> I think we've always lived with this tension, haven't we? You know trying to define exactly "What is a deacon?" and "What is a presbyter?"
>
> **Respondent,** *Area Group G*

Even deacons who tried to draw firm distinctions between the ministries of deacons and presbyters then frequently then went on to recognise what these ministries had in common; e.g.:

> I often think that presbyters see themselves as the way they work as being diaconal in nature. There can be a bit of tension between us.
>
> **Respondent,** *Area Group P*

> What is the real definition of being presbyteral or diaconal? There are some presbyters who work in a diaconal way and this is what I'm struggling with.
>
> **Respondent,** *Area Group O*

Some deacons also recognised areas of potential overlap in appointments between deacons, presbyters and lay people:

> The appointments I've had . . . some of them you wouldn't necessarily say they are particularly specific to deacons. A number of them have been ones that both lay and presbyteral people do as well.
>
> **Respondent,** *Area Group J*

This same deacon later went on to illustrate the sort of difficulties that deacons often got into when trying (and frequently failing) to explain the nature of any differences between ways of working in a coherent manner:

> I think there is something that a deacon has, that a presbyter does as well and lay people in the Church . . . I think there is something about being, by the nature of diaconal appointments, a reflective practitioner. That means you can reflect upon what, where and how your circumstances will mean that you will serve. So there is something about being able to do that. There is something about being able to contextualize where you are at that time and what that

means and how then you bring your diaconal ministry into that.
Again I still think this is something for presbyters as well.

Respondent, *Area Group J*

Any attempt to define the difference between the roles in terms of *particular tasks* that deacons either did or did not do also failed to capture the distinction between roles. Many of the particular activities that deacons mentioned themselves as doing within a typical week might equally be done by presbyters and/or lay people. For example, the deacons interviewed regularly mentioned activities such as preaching, taking a funeral, starting a Sunday night youth service, or providing pastoral care for members of a local congregation. Areas of work such as chaplaincy provided particular areas of overlap. Indeed, any approach to defining either order of ministry within the Methodist Church by what made it unique tended to be problematic, reducing complex and overlapping ministries to caricatures.

A number of deacons lamented the fact that they were frequently defined by what they cannot do. For instance, one deacon noted that they often heard people describing a deacon's ministry in this way:

> They know deacons don't preside [at Eucharist] and they know deacons will not . . . and it was all about what we don't do. Every single sentence . . .

Respondent, *Area Group L*

Within such definitions, issues such as who presides at Eucharist take on particular symbolic as well as practical significance in differentiating between ordained ministries (see Box A on the following page).

Given such difficulties in defining themselves in other ways, there was a tendency for deacons to return to citing their membership of the Methodist Diaconal Order *as a religious order* as the defining characteristic of their collective identity that distinguished them both from presbyters and from lay people. This had strong historic roots, as the remainder of this chapter will now explore. It also had a significant impact on their self-understanding, mutual support, interactions with others, and approaches to tackling the learning needed to respond to diverse and changing circumstances, as Chapter 7 will explore.

BOX A: DEACONS AND EUCHARISTIC PRESIDENCY

In the Methodist Church in Britain, Eucharistic Presidency is a particular aspect of a presbyter's role undertaken on behalf of the Methodist Conference which can only be undertaken by a deacon in exceptional circumstances and with special authorisation by the Conference. It therefore has a particularly symbolic significance and importance in questions of distinguishing the two orders of ministry within this Church, and in defining their inter-relationship. During the project period, issues of Eucharistic Presidency were being debated within the Connexion. The Methodist Diaconal Order's Convocation returned to discuss these issues twice in different years, with deacons holding particularly diverse views on whether they should be allowed to preside in some circumstances or not.[14]

Many deacons did not wish to be allowed to preside at Eucharist and many commented that this was part of what confirmed their personal call to become a deacon. However, some deacons raised particular issues around Eucharist if they felt that occasionally being able to preside was integral to their ministry to people who were on the edges in the various ways described earlier in this book. Key examples of this noted in the research included when:

1. in ministering to people on the edge of the church (e.g. in chaplaincy roles in hospital), there were occasionally situations (e.g. when someone they visited turned out to be dying) when deacons would have liked to share communion, but they had not taken extended communion with them, and a presbyter would not arrive in time. (However, one deacon commented that, in the particular instance of hospitals, hospital chaplaincy teams often have reserved sacrament kept for this purpose).

2. deacons had been stationed by Conference to minister to congregations in situations where these congregations would otherwise be deprived of communion because of their isolated situation (e.g. sparsely populated large rural Circuits where the presbyter/s in the Circuit were spread too thinly). Deacons had been asked by Conference to take on quasi-presbyteral roles in such Circuits in the past, particularly in situations when there had been a shortage of presbyters available. In such circumstances, the justification of "exceptional need" had been historically used by Conference to grant temporary permission to deacons performing roles in these contexts. The situations where this was needed were noted as having now reduced considerably.

3. deacons were involved in developing Fresh Expressions of Church which were at a critical stage in their development, when their relationships with those attending were crucial to how this fresh expression of church had developed, and where bringing in a presbyter who those attending didn't know felt problematic.

Such examples raised particular issues in terms of deacons' collaborative working with presbyters and their desire to respond to the needs of the Church and those with whom they were working. The underlying issues, however resolved, also had particularly wide-ranging implications for ecumenical discussions.

6.3.3.   The Impact of History on a Deacon's Identity

Underlying these debates about respective roles and tasks was a widespread frustration held by many deacons about the extent to which their ministry was recognised *in practice* as equal to that of their presbyteral colleagues. Former reports presented to the Methodist Conference had emphasised the equality of status of the diaconate with other forms of ministry within the Church. For example, the report *What is a Deacon?* accepted by Methodist Conference in 2004 recognised that "the Church should be a community of mutual support and love in which there is no superiority or inferiority". An earlier working party report on the diaconate which was originally presented to the 1997 Conference[15] indicated that:

> 1.2 The working party has consistently been guided by the belief that Methodism regards lay, diaconal and presbyteral ministries as having different identities and emphases but equal value. Diaconal ministry within Methodism is neither of lower nor of higher status than presbyteral ministry. Nor is its nature such that deacons and deaconesses should be excluded from any sphere of ministry which may properly be exercised by both presbyters and lay people. Provision has therefore to be made for deaconesses and deacons to serve on committees, hold senior office, be members of the Conference, preach, and so on.[16]

However, this official position did not necessarily reflect many deacons' experiences of the way they felt they were treated and regarded by many of those within local churches. Many deacons shared a particularly intense frustration with the frequency with which they were asked by congregation members: "When are you going to become a '*proper* minister'?"

The implication perceived of such comments was that deacons' present ministry was somehow improper or second-rate. This was frequently set within recounted narratives of how the Methodist Church had developed and changed in its treatment of this ministry historically. The impact of historical struggles for deacons to be recognised as equal ministers was frequently cited as adding to tensions that were inherent in the deacons' roles as described in earlier sections.[17]

This experience is better understood when set critically in the context of substantial wider historical evidence about the way this ministry has been treated previously by the Church. Early clashes between different ministries contributed towards the diaconate having a reduced role for much of the Church's history, to the detriment of the Church as a whole.[18] The early experiments of Christians in the nineteenth century, seeking to respond to the changed social and economic circumstances of these times, led to the re-emergence of a range of renewed diaconal movements.[19] In this context, a number of different early deaconess movements in Methodism enabled single Christian women to organise responses to the pressing social and spiritual needs of the day.[20] The Wesley Deaconess Order formed from a combination of these, and continued until latterly becoming the current Methodist Diaconal Order. One deacon linked the establishment of these earlier movements to the resurgence of interest in the diaconate in the current context, including the reformation into the current Order, as both happened during periods of rapid social change:

> I think the relationship between [then and] where we are now, when the change is going on—to me, I see that as a response to the changing world . . . I think that . . . if you look over history, that's where diaconal ministry often fits in and comes to the fore, when there is a change. I mean, I'm thinking [that the] Industrial Revolution was when deaconesses were suddenly thrown in. They suddenly arose in recent history because of the dramatic changes that were going on and they went and they dealt with all the poverty and the poor conditions that the Industrial Revolution had thrown up.
>
> **Respondent,** *Area Group G.*

The early deaconesses engaged in as wide a range of roles as their counterparts do today. For example, a report on the work of deaconesses that was presented to the Wesleyan Methodist Conference in 1902–3 listed a wide range of potential roles:

> The Work of the Deaconess is very varied. She may be a *Church Deaconess*, aiding in the pastoral work of a great congregation . . . a *Mission Deaconess* . . . a *Deaconess-Evangelist* . . . a *Deaconess-Nurse* . . . a *Deaconess Teacher* . . . a *Slum Deaconess*, caring for the very lowest; or she may be the *trusted friend*, and humanly speaking, the saviour of women who are lost in the midst of wealth and fashion. She may be engaged in *Rescue* work for women or for the prisoner, working at the prison-gate or within the prison. And lastly she may be a *Foreign Missionary Deaconess*.[21]

As will be apparent from the accounts in the earlier sections of this book, this work has changed over time, as deaconesses responded flexibly to the changing demands of the Methodist Church as well as different contexts and historical periods.[22] To take just one example, stations as foreign missionaries have declined over time as the focus has shifted to work in the UK and foreign branches of the Methodist Church have established their own structures. Another example is the changing role in healthcare, where involvement no longer takes the form of direct nursing roles, and has increasingly taken the form of chaplaincy, as nursing roles have become professionalised and state involvement increased.

Indeed, it was arguably because of their high degree of flexibility in roles and fluidity of identity that deaconesses, and latterly deacons, were able to adapt and maintain the bridging nature of their work in the midst of these rapidly-changing contexts. Within this work and context, the structure and fellowship of the Order provided a hugely significant framework for organising and supporting these deaconesses in their ministry. It also provided a common source of collective identity in the midst of the diverse and changing nature of their work, which continued to the present period: "We all have a calling to serve, so probably at the end of the day, I have to say for me, it's belonging to a religious order [that distinguishes us from others]" (Respondent, *Area Group H*).

Deacons also suggested that these substantial changes in role were not about just responding to significant social changes, but also to changes occurring within the Methodist Church. One particularly significant change was the opening of presbyteral ministry to women, which preceded the decision by the Methodist Church to cease recruiting new deaconesses in 1978.[23] Talking about this time, one former deaconess commented:

> It's an interesting point that when women were allowed into the presbyteral ministry and the Order was strongly reduced in numbers, quite a few ministers just expected that we'd all go [and become presbyters] and some of us said "No"! And that was quite a shock to them.
>
> **Respondent, *Area Group G***

Another commented that she hadn't become a presbyter at this time because she "didn't feel called to presbyteral ministry; it's as simple as that!" (Respondent, *Area Group G*).

This created a period of substantial turmoil for those within the Wesley Deaconess Order, which took some time to resolve, as the Church engaged in widespread debate. For the deaconesses in the midst of this, their ministry was felt to be challenged and its existence threatened, until:

> The female-only Wesley Deaconess Order was reformed by the
> Methodist Conference of 1986 into what became known from 1988
> as the Methodist Diaconal Order.[24] The Methodist Diaconal Order
> included all of the previous Wesley Deaconesses, and accepted new
> candidates irrespective of whether they were male or female (with
> both becoming referred to as "deacons").[25]

However, it was only in 1998 that the process came to completion by
which Methodism came to acknowledge that it had received from God an
order of deacons in the universal Church. In that year, all deacons were
received into full Connexion with the Conference, thus being authorised
in the same way as presbyters to exercise their ordained ministry in the
Methodist Church.[26]

This history and development of the Wesley Deaconess Order/
Methodist Diaconal Order has had a profound impact on the development
of deacons' identity, relationships, support structures and practices in the
contemporary context. Current deacons often talked about this history
with each other, and some recognised that it continued to have an impact
on their current practice. For example, one commented:

> I've always carried it with me and I think, we do bring an awful lot
> of the gifts of the Wesley deaconesses, but I think we can carry a
> bit of their baggage too.
>
> **Respondent,** *Area Group H*

Given that the data collected for this research was collected from deacons
who had been members of the Order for varying lengths of time, much of
it was potentially shaped by experiences dating back many years. However,
deacons continued to report some negative attitudes being shown to
deacons in the contemporary context which had developed from this
historical experience, despite changes in official Methodist Church policy.
These accounts were observed to be circulating amongst deacons; for
example, one newer deacon asked in an area group:

> Has anyone had any resistance from some of the Reverends? I know
> a deacon that I did a placement with had said that one of her friends
> when she had been ordained her first placement, the Reverend, the
> presbyter she worked with was very old and said to her: "I don't

recognise deacons or [the] diaconate . . . I don't recognise your ordination at all and I'm not really happy about you being here." As a first, very first [experience at a] place of ministry or training! . . . Have you guys come across that much?

Respondent, *Area Group U*

This history has developed over a number of years within the context of the wider Methodist Church and in the context of a wider society that often had very patriarchal values, in which women were viewed as second-class citizens. Because the history of the Order is bound up in this wider gendered context, there are numerous examples of the ways that this has affected deacons' perceptions of themselves and affected the ministry of deacons—and particularly deaconesses—over time. When deacons spoke about the history of the Order, one of the themes that emerged was that the Wesley deaconesses had represented a more uniform and subservient order of ministry in the Church:

> I mean people sort of have the image of the Wesley deaconess, but it was at times a rather subservient image—that the Wesley deaconess was there to pick up the pieces and to do the dirty work and to be the sort of assistant.
>
> **Male Respondent, *Area Group T***

One respondent spoke of how they all were simply called "sister" without being recognised as having a specific name, while another stressed how:

> There was more of an assumption in the old Wesley Deaconess Order that you could be interchangeable—that you could fit into each other shoes—than there is now.
>
> **Respondent, *Area Group H***

What is more, the interviewees' narrations of the past included references to the deaconesses being "cheap labour", alongside accounts that they were "hard done by" and "treated very poorly" (Respondent, *Area Group P*). There were times when a range of different deacons recalled feeling collectively marginalised, using words such as "overlooked", "second class", "treated as not quite the same", "not included", and "pushed down and left out". There was additional empirical evidence relating to this; for example, it is only comparatively recently that the standards required for housing deacons were brought into line with those for presbyters, and deaconesses who married were not allowed to continue working but took on a status of "married without appointment" until 1966. One interviewee who had lived through this period even noted earlier understandings of deaconesses that supposed "the women who were called should not be a financial liability to the Church" (Respondent, *Area Group G*). As a result, there was a time early in this history when deaconesses were only paid expenses.[27]

Arguably, similar critical questions might be asked about the different historical structures inherited from a previous period when there were male presbyters and female deaconesses. One example of these is the closer direct control vested in the Warden (who for much of the Wesley Deaconess Order's history was a male presbyter who oversaw the ministry of the women in the Order).[28] Another example is the more limited scope that deaconesses (and now, to a lesser extent, deacons) had to express preferences in the process that decides where their appointments might be. This arose as a result of the Methodist Church's understanding of "direct stationing" for deacons/deaconesses, which imposed higher expectations on deaconesses than presbyters to go where they were sent. In both of these cases, though, deacons and deaconesses before them have arguably made a virtue of serving despite differential (even discriminatory) structures and processes. Indeed, they have used these structures and processes to provide a particular contribution to the Church that spoke theologically and prophetically through this service whilst supporting each other.

Deacons interviewed also frequently pointed to the way that certain deacons had historically been required by the Methodist Church to take on presbyteral responsibilities, which had further undervalued and confused the wider Methodist Church's understanding of the particular focus that deacons brought to their work. This was reflected in an exchange between two deacons in one of the area groups:

> It's a bit difficult really, because the whole situation is so different. In the 1970s, we were cheap ministers. We were paid less, we went where they couldn't get a minister.[29] In the '80s and '90s, I would say that I was a substitute minister. Paid more, but because there weren't enough diaconal appointments, I was in presbyteral appointments

so that ... you know this distinction between diaconate and presbyteral has been irrelevant [at times] in ministry.

First respondent, *Area Group C*

I can echo that. Most of the time that I was in full time, I was doing pseudo-presbyteral work because that is what the Church demanded. And they would pay lip service to a deacon, but when push came to shove and the job needed doing, you do it and the finer points of diaconal ministry and presbyteral ministry were completely forgotten.

Second respondent, *Area Group C*

In the midst of these narrations, familiar accounts of conflicts between deacons and presbyters emerged, with one interviewee referencing a series of past correspondence in the Methodist Recorder which suggested that historically, when there had been a conflict between a presbyter and a deaconess, "it's always the deaconess that moves" (Respondent, *Area Group R*). One instance where these themes were explored further was in consultation discussions on diaconal ministry sponsored by the Joint Implementation Commission[30] that were observed during the research process. The report written by Charlton to reflect these discussions to the Joint Implementation Commission following this event noted that:

> Within both Churches, it was acknowledged that diaconal ministry can be disabled by presbyteral colleagues ... This is especially true when the full breadth and potential of diaconal ministry is misunderstood or seen to be subordinate within a group of ministers. Diaconal work is most effective when deacons are trusted, released and given permission to take risks.[31]

6.3.4.   The Impact of this History on Contemporary Deacons' Ministries

This chequered and multifaceted history had a wide range of perceived implications for deacons' contemporary ministry. Importantly, the previous uses and abuses of a deacon's ministry as servant ministry were seen as having particular implications for contemporary deacons' practice. Some deacons recognised that they needed to reflect particularly carefully on their theology of how they engaged critically with issues of power and status as a result, and encourage the wider Church to do this too. The consultation discussion between the Church of England and the Methodist Church on diaconal ministry that was sponsored by the Joint Implementation Commission, referred to at the end of the previous section, illustrates these issues well. Within the report based on these discussions, Charlton notes that deacons also need to reflect on how they model Jesus as a servant leader—learning from how he dealt with being in the position of a servant, and used this to challenge the perceptions of those around him:

> Throughout the consultation, and especially in conversations about leadership, there was a distinction drawn between understandings of "service" and "servant". The deacons strongly resisted images of Jesus (and through this their own self-identity and vocation) as "meek and mild". Jesus came to serve and radically inverted power relationships by choosing to serve. That choice did not make him a slave to what everyone around him told him to do, or a servant of their every whim. There is a distinction between such servility and freely given service as a measure of love for others and God's love for us. Service that is chosen is very different from the concept of bound service inherent within being unable to get out of the powerless role of being a servant. The Gospel may be incarnationally embodied in the choice to give service, not out of compulsion or servility, but born of free will—and not in a philanthropic sense of doing good to others, but out of identifying with them. Although clearly the role of Christian obligation and Paul's insistence in using the vocabulary of slavery as the background for all roles within the Christian Church needs to be kept in mind.[32]

In identifying those who are excluded and marginalised, there is an inherent risk that deacons can become stuck "on the edge" themselves. In light of this potential danger, it becomes especially important that deacons keep moving around the loop pictured previously in Figure 1 (p. 66). By doing this, they can avoid becoming stuck in an identity that is solely concerned with being marginalised or a victim. Instead, by keeping moving, they can constantly weave through these various contexts and thus make connections back to the wider Church. The Joint

Implementation Commission-sponsored discussions saw this as fitting within an understanding of "what authority was given to deacons, by whom and for what tasks":

> For both Churches [The Methodist Church in Britain and the Church of England], the response to this question arises from a common understanding that the calling is God's work in the lives of the individuals and He bestows authority to others. The ministry of those ordained deacon is owned by the church, who then releases deacons into a representative work for the Kingdom, on behalf of others, and in accord with individual gifts and graces. There is a sense of the church giving, empowering and releasing: the picture is of a strong elastic tether that enables people to be sent out, let out yet with a connection that can support and pull back. Deacons work with a sense of personal autonomy and under the oversight of others, both in response to a calling from God within the context of a known tradition and structure.[33]

This location, authorisation and continued connection within the Church's structure were important, as the quotation above acknowledges. However, the historical experiences of deacons within churches have not always reflected this continuing support and recognition, and where this was lacking it was seen to have substantially undermined their work. The fact that the Wesley Deaconess Order had been closed to recruitment for a period, with some deaconesses told to find themselves secular appointments, had left some deacons feeling particularly hurt and under-recognised. These deaconesses remained part of the Order when it was re-opened for recruitment and subsequently renamed, and formed the majority of its members throughout its initial years. This was combined with the Methodist Church's evolving understanding of this ministry as being recognised as an Order of Ministry, which meant that many of the deacons had lived through a period where their recognition and status as an ordained minister had been questionable. These accounts were set in a broader context of deacons recognising that the situation in the present day was very different, albeit still affected by some continuing effects from the historical context. For example:

> I think there's probably challenges faced by deacons that are not
> faced by presbyters in that, because the Order is changing—it's
> growing in size—that the general church community are not always
> up to speed, if you like . . . Historically . . . deacons have gone to
> Circuits and people don't really know what they're getting, in terms
> of they don't understand the nature of diaconal ministry . . . I think
> people experience colleagues that don't understand the nature of
> a deacon, and you find yourself—certainly I did—I almost had to
> prove my worth . . . I think I was viewed on by some as a bit of an
> expensive lay worker.
>
> **Respondent,** *Area Group C*

In this context, deacons were very conscious that others sometimes
perceived them as somehow in-between a lay and ordained status, despite
having been officially recognised as ordained. This historical position
between presbyters and lay people meant that deacons often had to struggle
with others to locate themselves accurately and find their place amongst
the other ministries in the Church. One deacon expressed this difficulty
well in saying:

> You're neither [seen as] minister nor lay are you? You're somewhere
> in no man's land. That does happen, I've friends now who struggle,
> really struggle in their appointments because they don't have the
> colleagueship and they can't find their place.
>
> **Respondent,** *Area Group P*

Whilst now recognised by Conference as an order of ministry in the
same way as presbyters, the relatively recent nature of this change was
also indicated by continuing efforts to make legal changes to foundational
documents in order to recognise deacons' ministries appropriately.[34]
Deacons were keen to claim and retain their comparatively recent
equality of status, and often frustrated when they were not recognised in
this way by those within churches. However, at the same time, the way
that their position was seen by some as having a different, more liminal
status with regards to ordination (in comparison with presbyters) was also
sometimes helpful in supporting them in playing a different role within
congregations. For example, one deacon recognised that whilst she was
equally as ordained as her presbyter colleague, lay members within church

communities did not necessarily see it that way. She spoke of how people related to her in a different way, seeing her as more approachable:

> People talk to me and tell me things that they don't tell him . . . and it's not just to do with being a woman or to do with my . . . personality . . . [One person explained why they saw me as more approachable by saying "Your presbyteral colleague] is holy, and you're almost holy!"

These differing perceptions of congregational members, whether or not they reflected official Church teaching or the views of deacons themselves, held open the possibility of people talking to deacons about problems or issues about which they might not talk to others. Because some people saw them as less set apart from the rest of the congregation than presbyters, some deacons said that members of congregations saw deacons as more like them. As a result, these members of congregations had said to deacons that they saw them as able to come alongside them in a different way, to struggle with them as they sought to find ways to engage in forms of mission and service.

Another deacon linked this back to the controversial issue of dress by stating:

> Ever since I have been in the Order, I have been very anti-wearing a dog collar, but I am absolutely convinced that I would only have to wear it once and they would see me differently here. It's quite interesting, but it's because you don't wear a dog collar, they don't see you as a minister.
>
> **Respondent, *Area Group U***

In such situations, wearing the clerical collar (or taking on other tasks or traits traditionally associated with presbyters) was seen in an ambivalent way. This was because to do so was seen as both helping to gain recognition from the congregation, whilst at the same time having a lasting impact in destroying the ambiguity of an alternative position that enabled deacons to play a different role within that congregation.

There were also other areas of the Methodist Church's life which indicated evidence of continued institutional wrestling with how to recognise this liminal role appropriately. For example, there were significant debates over the Vice-Presidency of Conference during the project period. This leadership role has traditionally been available to either a deacon or lay person, whilst the Presidency is a presbyteral role. In many of these debates, the deacon's position was recognised as neither presbyter nor lay, and hence uncomfortably disrupted structures and categories in the wider Church. A Senior Leadership Review and the election of a deacon to the Vice-Presidency during the research period brought to the surface continuing debates across the Connexion about whether this might displace lay people from these senior positions. Such debates were reported as recurring whenever a deacon has been elected to this position. These discussions stimulated a range of debates about the nature of leadership in the Church, and various proposals were made to reform the structure of the presidency in response to this. In 2011, this eventually resulted in much of the traditional structure being reaffirmed in principle, whilst making additional provision for the President and Vice-President to share duties more extensively and work more collaboratively.[35]

The involvement of some deacons in preaching was another example of a role that unsettled the boundaries/categories—because those deacons that did preach were understood to do so by virtue of their status as a local preacher (alongside lay colleagues), rather than because it was inherently within their role as an ordained order of ministry (as it was for presbyters).

By upsetting clear-cut categories between presbyters and lay people in instances such as these, the deacon's role stimulated continued debate and reflection about important issues such as the nature of ministry, ordination and leadership.

6.3.5. Deacons & Presbyters: Differing Foci, Complementary Collaboration

Understanding the creative nature of the liminal identity and role occupied by deacons was crucial to understanding their potential to make connections between the various aspects of their work. Indeed, it was their ability to move between different domains and connect them that was central to the ways that they supported the Church's participation in God's mission. Where relationships between deacons and presbyters were polarised in practice, this frequently caused conflicts and problems in achieving the connections that made for effective diaconal ministry as outlined in Chapters 3, 4 and 5. However, where these ordained ministries worked in a complementary and relational way, adapting their interface according to the needs of particular contexts, they were seen as much more effective. One deacon described this relationship in terms of "crossover" between these ordained ministries, where "the presbyter crosses a little bit into [the deacon's ministry], and we cross a little bit into [the presbyter's ministry]" (Respondent, *Area Group E*).

Within this relationship, analysis of the data suggests that the divisions between deacons and presbyters are porous and permeable in nature, and as such these ministries are not separated into completely distinctive groups of tasks. Instead, they share aspects of their practices and roles, whilst still having distinct foci. This stands in contrast to any insistence that a deacon and presbyter's role is established by a rigid boundary; indeed, as one deacon commented, a stark contrast between "black and white doesn't work" (Respondent, *Area Group D*).

Instead, the boundary between these different identities and ministries is a hazy zone of transition rather than a clear line indicating where discrete identities and ministries begin and end. Within this transitional zone, permeable boundaries of collaboration are then negotiated between those involved, in ways that are appropriate to particular contexts.

Recognising the importance of this collaboration and the overlapping nature of these ministries leaves room for them to each have a distinct focus, whilst at the same time enabling both to operate together in all contexts within churches and wider communities. The distinctiveness in the foci perhaps lies in the differing proportions of time and energy spent within different contexts, and the way that these ministries come at these contexts as a result.

Indeed, because the ministry is as much part of who the deacon or presbyter is as what they do, even when they do tasks which would normally be within each other's role, some deacons tended to feel that they might approach such tasks from a somewhat different angle:

> Even if a deacon does a lot more presbyteral work, I think they do it different to a presbyter, because they're being a deacon and there's something in that. And the same with a presbyter who is more in the community, they do it different to a deacon I think.
>
> **Respondent, *Area Group E***

Some deacons had particular skills or experience in working in particular places on the loop indicated in Figure 1 (p. 66), such as those who had previously worked in setting up pioneering ministries within wider communities on new housing estates where there was no church building. Others had particular skills and experience at the other extreme of this loop, for example mainly having worked within large congregations doing pastoral support work alongside colleagues who were presbyters, or having worked when required by Conference to fill quasi-presbyteral roles to cover historic presbyter shortages.

Whether or not deacons actually "do it different[ly]", the idea of a differing "focus" to the ministry of presbyters and deacons, with permeable boundaries of collaboration that are negotiated in particular contexts, fitted the data much better than an entirely distinct set of roles. As one contributor who was not a deacon commented that "the respective foci of these ministries reveal more clearly to the Church what its calling and ministry is, representing together what all Christians are called to do".

The crucial issue was how these roles were negotiated in relationship with presbyters and those engaged in other forms of ministry within particular contexts. As a presbyter who was a member of the Methodist Church's Connexional Team commented during the research:

> I think the issue is not where you place the boundary but what kind of boundary you place. That's what my view is. So I think [drawing too clear a line between presbyter and deacon] is a false dichotomy and I can see why [some people say it should be a dichotomy], but I think it's a dangerous one. If you are too vague, then you also lose the possibility of being useful. So I would have lots of ethical questions similarly. I think it's much wiser in my view to define tightly but have gentle boundaries, rather than to have loose-limbed, inelegant, vastly complicated, distant boundaries which are impenetrable. I mean the ideal boundary in my humble opinion is a cell wall which is precisely designed to let things cross it—that's what it's designed for. And I think the cell wall boundary of an organic kind, when the whole purpose of what defines a deacon and what doesn't define a deacon is a boundary precisely which allows flexibility across it, is much wiser than trying to draw infinitely complicated loose-limbed one so you've got both the identity but also the possibility of movement.

This quotation captures well the tensions and questions which remain, as well as indicating a potentially helpful direction for future development. It was not possible to explore further how these ministries see themselves as fitting together without doing similar research with presbyters about how they understand their own ministries and how they see these relating to the ministries of deacons and others. Such research would be a helpful next step to continue this process, and hence this forms one of the recommendations arising from this research[36].

KEY QUESTIONS

1. How should the Church understand the relationship between the different ministries, both ordained and lay, within the Church today?
2. In what ways should different roles overlap, and in what ways might their different contributions best be understood?
3. (a) To what extent have the Church's contemporary understandings about respective roles and structures been shaped by historical understandings? (b) Which of these, if any, should be critically reviewed in order to better reflect the Gospel?

6.4.   CHAPTER 6 CONCLUSION

One crucial issue identified by deacons was the way in which deacons and presbyters work together and negotiate their relationship within a particular context. Where these relationships worked well, they were seen as depending on:

- Mutual recognition of each other's foci; *combined with*
- Good relationships that allowed links to be made between each other's work; *and*
- Flexibility in negotiations over how roles were shared between diverse ministry teams (including lay and ordained people).

In the everyday experiences of ministry, circumstances can make combining these aspects a difficult balance to achieve, and this formed the nature of some common dilemmas faced by deacons. For example, one deacon recounted how a presbyter colleague had sacrificially made room for this to happen:

> I was very lucky in coming to my present appointment because the presbyter was absolutely determined that my appointment would be a diaconal appointment even to the extent where he was overworked and had lost a presbyter colleague, he still wouldn't let me help him and do presbyteral work because he wanted the church to see that there was a difference in roles. And I thought that was a very gracious thing for him to do because I know he was working so hard. I had quite a lot of free time but he wanted me to develop the diaconal work and not be helping him. I found that a very gracious thing to do.
>
> **Respondent,** *Area Group U*

The dilemma in this situation for the deacon was how to support a colleague flexibly in difficult, pressured circumstances whilst still making space for the differing foci of their own roles. This needed to be a two-way interaction, in which deacons also expected to support presbyter colleagues where it was appropriate to the context, as another deacon made clear:

> I do see my role as making sure that my presbyteral colleagues are able to do their work well, and if there are things that I can do that will enable them to have a freedom [in their ministry], then I will try and do that.
>
> **Respondent,** *Area Group H*

The deacons' responses noted that where these relationships worked best, they were part of a picture in which there is a broader team-based approach to ministry. Within the effective teams described, flexible and negotiated boundaries combined with recognition of those responsibilities and duties as Christians that are shared among deacons, presbyters and lay people. This involved recognising and making space for the contributions of lay people alongside these ordained ministries, and working closely together with them. It also involved recognising the particular contributions that each of these groups can make, valuing their contribution to the whole.

NOTES

1. The word "liminal" derives from the Latin word for "threshold", and refers to being on the margin between places or being in a transitional period (Oxford English Dictionary). These marginal or transitional spaces have particular potential to unsettle the otherwise clear/firm socially-defined categories around them. It has been developed as a significant theoretical concept by a range of writers, particularly in the discipline of anthropology. It has been applied particularly to deacons by authors such as MacRae 2009 (esp. Ch. 2) in describing the "de-centred ministry" of deacons, and Brown 2005 p. xiii, who refers to deacons as "liminal people who are comfortable living on boundaries".

2. Cf. For this denomination, both *What is a Deacon?* (Methodist Church in Britain 2004) and *What is a Presbyter?* (Methodist Church in Britain 2002) reports, as agreed by the Methodist Church at Conference.

3. It is important to note that not all deacons would necessarily have agreed with extending diaconal ministry to those "who don't name the name of Christ"; some set it more in the context of developing discipleship and working in tune with the Holy Spirit who is already active in the wider world, including amongst non-Christians.

4. These two words reflect two distinct senses of usage derived from the Greek word *diakonia* (and related words) in Biblical texts. One sense is as a word in general usage, adopted to describe something in which the whole Church was called to be involved (what we have called "diaconal ministry" throughout this book), and the other (later) sense is in terms of a particular office beginning within the early Church (what we have called "deacon" throughout this report). See Gooder 2006, for a summary of related debates.

5. A critical analysis of the understanding of the diaconate in British Methodism in a comparative ecumenical context as developed through this research project can be found in Orton 2012.

6. See Chapter 4, footnote 5 for a further explanation of these initiatives.

7. Throughout this quotation, to maintain confidentiality, "Heather" is a pseudonym.

8. See Appendix D.

9. During the research, despite not adopting a research strategy which sought to engage with wider congregations within the data collection stage of this project, the researchers were aware of more than one person who would have liked to candidate as a "local deacon" if this were an option. For example, one person proactively approached the research team during the project in response to the conference publicity to ask whether this was under consideration. They cited the "Local Preacher" role as a possibly similar model already existing within this denomination which could be drawn on in developing a "local deacon" role in the Methodist Church.

10. For example, many other religious orders (e.g. the Society of St Francis) have associated "third orders" which enable lay people to participate within them in some way. There is currently a category of "associate membership" of the Order which consists mainly of those former deaconesses who became presbyters when presbyteral ministry became available to them. There has recently been an internal consultation within the Order about deacons' perspectives on this category of membership. There were previous discussions within Conference about whether a religious order which extended beyond those ordained as a deacon might be helpful in enabling lay diaconal ministry, which took place when the Methodist Diaconal Order was first established in its current form. Former Warden of the Order Sue Jackson asked whether the Order was now "a mature enough community to accept the challenge of exploring whether we are at another *kairos* moment. Are we being called to embrace a wider cross-section of people, equally passionate about living out a spirituality of *diakonia* . . . ?" (Jackson 2008, p. 169, emphasis as in original, with the spelling of "kairos" corrected here from "kyros" in the original). The General Secretary's report to the 2011 Conference indicated that the Methodist Church would need to explore more flexible options for forms of local ministry in the contemporary context, whether ordained (as presbyter or deacon) or not. All of these indicate some possible ways of exploring these questions further.

11. This approach to deacons defining themselves as opposed to presbyters was found in 115 references within 19 different area groups.

12. Methodist Church in Britain 2004.

13. Methodist Church in Britain 2002.

14. Given the controversial and ongoing nature of this debate, and the wide range of views, it is important to note that this book does not attempt to discuss comprehensively all deacons' perspectives on this issue, nor comment on the Methodist Diaconal Order's collective evaluation and official position

on them. Instead, it includes some examples which are relevant to the wider themes discussed here.

15. *The Diaconate*, report presented to the 1997 Methodist Conference, reprinted in Methodist Church in Britain 2000, pp. 323–346; the following quote is from p. 323 of this collection.

16. Subsequently, the term "deacon" became used in an inclusive way to include both men and women.

17. These important issues have been explored in more detail in relation to wider literature, including a further analysis of the important gender dimension to this history, in Orton 2012.

18. Barnett 1981; O'Toole 1992.

19. Staton 2001.

20. Staton 2001; Graham 2002.

21. These roles are as recorded in the Wesley Deaconess Institute Mission Book 1895–1910, pp. 157–158, cited in Graham 2002, p. 8, (capitalisation as in the original).

22. Staton 2001; Graham 2002.

23. Methodist Church in Britain, Minutes of Conference, 1978, p. 29.

24. Staton 2001, pp. 257–299.

25. Orton 2012, p. 267.

26. Methodist Church in Britain 2004, p. 15.

27. Staton 2001, p. 115.

28. Sister Yvonne Hunkin was the first Deaconess Warden, taking up this role from 1980–1984, having been Associate Warden previously between 1977–1980. At the time of the appointment of the first three Deaconess Wardens, there remained a male Ministerial Secretary who represented the Order on Connexional Committees.

29. At the time that this deacon refers to, the term "minister" was used to mean "presbyter". The Methodist Church resolved in 2008 that the term "minister" was to be used more inclusively, to include presbyters and deacons, so this quote from a deacon who ministered through these changes is historically accurate, if not in keeping with contemporary usage. Legal changes which enabled this usage to be reflected in official documents were finally enacted by the Methodist Conference in 2012.

30. This consultation arose out of continuing discussions about the Church of England and Methodist Church in Britain working together more closely. The discussions were sponsored by the Joint Implementation Commission

set up by these two denominations, as part of the practical outworking of the Anglican-Methodist Covenant that was originally signed in 2003.

31. Charlton 2010, p. 12.

32. Charlton 2010, p. 3.

33. Charlton 2010, p. 12.

34. The doctrinal standards clause of the Deed of Union, clause 4, was amended slightly in 1995 (using the required two-year "special deferred resolution" procedure) so as to remove wording which might indicate that the Methodist Church had only one order of ordained ministry, i.e. the presbyteral. In 2010, the procedure was embarked upon again, this time explicitly to recognise deacons as an order of ministry within the Methodist Church; this was finally confirmed by Methodist Conference in 2012.

35. For full details, see the report *Leading and Presiding: Developing the Presidency of Conference* in the Methodist Conference Agenda 2011, p. 715–728.

36. See Recommendation 4 in Appendix E.

7. ENABLING EFFECTIVE GROWTH IN DEACONS' MINISTRIES: FORMATION, TRAINING, SUPPORT & CONTINUING LEARNING

7.1. INTRODUCTION TO CHAPTER 7

The previous chapters of this book have outlined the important contributions being made by deacons' ministries, whilst simultaneously highlighting how they can be incredibly challenging. This penultimate chapter explores the personal motivations that led deacons to commit to this lifelong ministry and the joys and challenges that deacons found within it. It also explores deacons' reflections on the process of formation, as well as the initial and ongoing sources of training and support that were available as they developed to respond to the challenges of their ministry. The analysis presented explores a number of factors identified within the findings that may contribute to and detract from a learning culture for deacons, as they minister within the context of the Methodist Diaconal Order and wider Church. The Methodist Diaconal Order's "Rule of Life" and its collective life as a religious order made crucial contributions within this process, and every aspect of this "Rule of Life" is considered in the course of the discussion.[1]

7.2. BEING A DEACON: THE PERSONAL MOTIVATIONS, JOYS AND CHALLENGES

Deacons spoke frequently of a deep personal sense of being called by God into being a deacon, as the accounts throughout this book testify. This personal calling had motivated them to offer themselves for this ministry, even when many found engaging in it a daunting prospect. As they grew in their experience, many deacons spoke of how they continued to find their life as a deacon both deeply challenging and profoundly rewarding. They frequently spoke passionately of the personal joy and enrichment to be found within their ministry, and counted it a privilege to participate in this work.

At the same time, deacons also shared how challenging and demanding this work can be. They identified a wide range of issues and dilemmas that they encountered within their practice. From personal feelings of inadequacy and frustration to emotional fatigue and busyness, deacons frequently pointed out the draining nature of their practice. Within this, the management of time and stress were major challenges they faced. These were particularly necessary given the challenges of this ministry and the often open-ended, never-ending nature of their potential work. This created particular challenges in designing particular appointments appropriately. Deacons frequently sought to retain the creative flexibility within an appointment to engage in opportunities as they were discerned. This meant that they had to manage a key tension between this space for discernment and needing to set some boundaries, such as by agreeing the focus of their contributions with Circuit Leadership Teams. This was particularly tricky for deacons when they first arrived in an appointment: at this time, they were trying to build new relationships and make space for a discernment process, whilst facing pre-determined expectations from the Circuit about what they would do and how they would do it. Well-designed appointments were considered to be those that made room for this and had some understanding of a deacon's role, whilst giving some focus for their engagement. Support from other ordained ministers and lay leaders was crucial to negotiating ways of working collaboratively and reasonable limits, as well as giving opportunities for collective review throughout the appointment as it developed.

Aspects of the "Rule of Life" were also important in managing these pressures, in encouraging deacons to be able stewards of their time, talents and resources. The "Rule of Life" particularly encouraged deacons to order the rhythm of their lives to allow for relaxation, study, a weekly day off and regular holiday. However, whilst deacons were sometimes observed to encourage each other in this, there were also numerous occasions where expectations of overwork were simply acknowledged amongst deacons as the norm, without being critiqued. A number of deacons noted that they had personally experienced times of "burning out" when these expectations had been absorbed and not been managed. In response, finding "ways of offloading" and carving out spaces for rest, reflection and listening to God emerged as an important practice for many deacons.

The importance of finding moments of humour within the work was also apparent within the observations conducted. These moments appeared to make a considerable contribution to relieving stress and helping the deacons to keep issues in perspective. Convocation provided examples of these strategies, making time for deacons to come together within the context of a programme designed to balance different opportunities for refreshing their ministry. This programme included frequent laughter and space for various activities designed to help deacons recharge being organised, alongside the more formal business, worship and learning sessions. One deacon described Convocation as "a real life-line", providing a key opportunity for deacons to reconnect to each other as a community. Both Convocations attended by the lead researcher included activities specifically designed to help deacons manage the stress of their work; for example, one plenary session was focused on how best to manage stress on an individual level. Deacons welcomed the general advice given, whilst indicating that they would benefit from developing strategies tailored to their own particular role, taking account of common expectations within local Circuits.

The "Rule of Life" includes a commitment to "be sensitive to the needs of those close to us, our families, dependents and friends". Deacons discussed dilemmas which had arisen for them when they recognised that the difficulties and challenges within their ministry were impacting on their own health and wellbeing, and that of their families. They also recognised that their own health and wellbeing and that of their families had sometimes impacted on their ministry. Some deacons discussed personally feeling emotional stress and physical fatigue from their ministry, using expressions such as "that first year in particular was just agony" (Respondent, *Area Group U*). The Order particularly sought to provide support to student deacons and probationer deacons to address this. This support included (for example) offering them particular advice during their Student Deacons' Conference on how to handle these issues, including on how to challenge unrealistic expectations constructively. However, there were also some occasions observed within the research where more experienced deacons informally passed on expectations of continual overwork to newer deacons. In the process, these were reinforced as simply being part of the culture of ministry in the Methodist Church, rather than being challenged.

A particular issue that came up repeatedly was the impact that itinerancy has upon deacons' families, and the dilemmas this created for them. For example, one deacon described her first move in the following way:

> My children had always come first and all of a sudden I was uprooting them. They came with me to a very, very difficult place for them. And it was right for me and I expected it to be right for them, that God would bless them if I was doing what He wanted me to. And to watch them go through absolute hell for probably a year because they so missed their friends and they were in another culture entirely as teenagers, broke my heart. I couldn't bear to see it and yet felt this was what God was calling me to do. It's not easy is it?
>
> **Respondent,** *Area Group U*

Other deacons described how their families' needs had caused dilemmas and limitations in terms of their availability to be stationed too far from a particular area, such as when they had caring responsibilities for elderly relatives. The Order's Leadership were aware of these issues, and care was observed to be taken in taking these family needs into account as far as possible. For example, deacons were encouraged to disclose family commitments that might limit their availability for stationing prior to the process. There was also space for family perspectives to be explicitly included in the process of making decisions about whether deacons should offer to stay in a particular place for a further term. Within the stationing process, the Warden made decisions about stationing in consultation with the Diaconal Stationing Sub-Committee (a sub-committee of the Connexional Stationing Committee). During one meeting of this sub-committee observed during the research, any personal and family needs which had been declared were taken into account as far as possible in recommending particular matches. These needs were observed as being treated as high priority considerations in deciding where particular deacons should be stationed. However, the limited number of stations available each year, and the challenges of matching multiple deacons to appointments that suited their gifts, meant that this was a complex exercise, in which deacons could not always be placed as closely as they might have liked. As Section 6.3.3 indicated, deacons also had to operate within a system of "direct stationing", which imposed on deacons a greater expectation that they would go where they were first sent, in comparison with the system used for stationing presbyters.[2] To support deacons in the challenges of this, one member of the Order Leadership Team had a role particularly dedicated to providing confidential pastoral support on a range of issues including stationing, alongside the peer support also available to everyone within the Order.

The time-limited nature of appointments within this system of itinerancy was seen by Deacons as having other effects on the potential of some of their ministry. Given the importance of the relational aspects of their ministry, which took time to develop, deacons sometimes felt they needed more time in their posts to see these relationships bear fruit. However, on a more positive note, deacons also recognised that the discipline of itinerancy focused their attention on trying to empower others within congregations to take up this ministry, because any specific deacon was not going to be around doing the role in one particular place forever.

KEY QUESTIONS

1. In what ways might different parts of the Church (including deacons themselves) help deacons to manage the potential sources of stress within their ministry?
2. In what ways can different parts of the Methodist Church contribute towards assuaging the challenges for deacons and presbyters arising from itinerancy?
3. How might Circuit profiles for Methodist deacons be designed in ways that show an understanding of a deacon's role in the way they set out expectations for particular appointments?

7.3. BELONGING TO THE ORDER: IDENTITY, SUPPORT, AND FORMATION

7.3.1. Reliant on God, Supported by the Order

In light of the challenges deacons faced, a number of deacons shared in the attitude of one who stressed the importance of "doing things in God's strength and not in my own strength" (Respondent, *Area Group Q*).

Deacons often directly linked their ability to respond to the range of local needs with their membership of the Methodist Diaconal Order as a religious order; for example:

> In your own strength, you would never either want to do it, or find you could do it. But because you are an Order and because you are there because you have been sent there and therefore God is in it, you know if you've got the power of God you can respond to need [even if] you didn't think you were able to.
>
> **Respondent, *Area Group N***

As this quotation illustrates, deacons drew strength from their belonging to the Order, and from the way they saw God sending them through the Church to serve and respond to need in diverse contexts. The common community of the Methodist Diaconal Order provided a source of support and belonging even whilst dispersed across different contexts. Deacons actively contributed to this community, including praying regularly for each other using a prayer diary. For example, one deacon commented:

> I think belonging to the Order is supreme, and so many things come from that, don't they? We have this togetherness . . . There is a strength that comes from belonging to each other that you don't have yourself.
>
> **Respondent, *Area Group N***

This was seen by deacons as vital given that the pressures of itinerancy could limit their sense of local belonging, and put pressures on them to keep changing and adapting who they were. One deacon described these pressures on their identity in the following way:

> It's a challenge because we are being put often into new opportunities for ministry . . . you are going into a totally different way of living or environment. My last place I lived on an estate, a rough estate in a council house—totally different to what I've been put into now. So you are facing new ways of living, new ways of being.
>
> **Respondent,** *Area Group M*

Whilst it was recognised that itinerant presbyters faced similar challenges, it was particularly vital for deacons given the particular stresses inherent in a ministry that involved bridging between different communities. As noted earlier, the nature of this ministry meant that deacons often found themselves located somewhere on the thresholds in between different people and places, not being completely in one place or another when trying to connect these different individuals, groups and places together. The Order's support was seen as crucial when such a ministry often left the deacons feeling that they did not wholly belong anywhere on a local level, despite relating closely to the multiple communities in which they lived. For example, one deacon indicated:

> I've not found a place really within the Circuit team, I feel very much on the fringe of that and on the fringe of the Circuit and so having the Order as a support, and knowing that I'm part of a community wider than that, has been really important to sustaining me while in that [local] community [feeling] isolated.
>
> **Respondent,** *Area Group J* [3]

As the previous chapters have illustrated, this potential for isolation was not just an issue about particular individuals' situations (although different individuals clearly did handle the tensions of this situation in different ways and with varying degrees of success). Instead, it was inherently related to the nature of a deacon's ministry in building bridges between diverse communities. As one deacon described it, the Order provided opportunities to ensure that support was "structured in more" to their collective life. It also meant that individual deacons could access support from outside their Circuit if they encountered difficulties in a particular appointment.

7.3.2.   A Collective Spirituality and Identity

Deacons also felt that the Order had been crucial in holding deacons together, especially whilst they had gone through the turbulent history described earlier in Sections 6.3.3 and 6.3.4. As one deacon commented:

> The Order has been ... sort of the glue that's held the deacons together, despite them being squashed this way and that way
>
> **Respondent,** *Area Group N*

In providing a common community which linked deacons together, the Order also helped nurture relationships in ways that deacons often struggled to describe well. This is well illustrated in the following quotation:

> It's the Order part, that our cords are almost like silk and threads drawn together, and you'll be closer to some than others, but when you meet, even those that you do not know that well, there is something in you that says "My heart speaks to your heart". Tangibly, I don't think I could ever put it on paper, but emotionally and awareness-wise [it's important] ... When I've been with the other members of the Order, I've had people meet me and ... they've said afterwards ... "What is it with you lot? You are so close!"
>
> **Respondent,** *Area Group H*

These common bonds and shared understandings were rooted in a collective spirituality which they consciously sought to nurture together:

> Recently, what's come home to me is that I can appreciate now more than ever, ever, ever what it means to belong to an Order, because I'm now into spirituality in a different way than I was before. And I think I've always taken for granted that spirituality stance that is part of the Order; therefore [it is] part of me, and continues to be part of me. And the spirituality that was given ... has become part of me without me realising it. [This] is something that's come home to me very recently, and I think that's very much an integral part of being a deacon.
>
> **Respondent,** *Area Group Q*

This collective spirituality was rooted in the model provided by the Order's "Rule of Life" (see Appendix D), which was frequently mentioned by deacons for the ways in which it contributed towards developing this collective spirituality. This "Rule of Life" included commitments to their collective life as a religious order, including attending Convocation, attending area groups and keeping in contact with each other, providing fellowship and mutual support. Deacons were frequently observed to be enquiring after each other's wellbeing, and commenting how much a phone call or card that they had received had meant to them during a time of difficulty. Supernumerary[4] deacons were active contributors to the Order, not least through the area groups and Convocation, and those able to be involved were valued participants who in turn valued this participation highly. This care also extended in a significant way to those deacons who had become incapacitated through illness or old age, through visits and other expressions of care. The "Rule of Life" combined this collective participation with individual actions to support their own devotional life, such as a commitment to attendance at worship, reading the Bible, praying and regular self-examination, and making time once a year to attend a retreat or quiet day. Deacons frequently mentioned these activities in the area groups observed, and often incorporated them into their collective life too, further helping to build their spiritual bond with each other.

Praying for one another was a particularly important aspect of this spiritual bond:

> We are within the Order as a function. But actually it's much deeper than that. It's a relationship but it's also a spirituality with being bound with praying for one another, and that's more of what it's about, rather than just a function.
>
> **Respondent,** *Area Group X*

> Our daily prayer for each other is something that's invaluable . . . We don't [always] know the results of it, except occasionally you get a letter or a card from somebody.
>
> **Respondent,** *Area Group N*

As this second quotation illustrates, as the Order had grown, deacons were not able to keep in touch personally with every member. However, resources such as prayer diaries that included all members helped to build wider awareness of each other, and the members' section of the Methodist Diaconal Order website helped deacons to be linked together systematically and communicate with each other collectively.

7.3.3.   A Shared Understanding that is "Caught, not Taught"?

This bond also included sharing some common understandings, and provided a safe place where deacons did not have to constantly explain themselves and who they were within their ministry. One deacon saw this as part of the way of life arising from being within this religious order, stating that "when we [within the Order] are saying things like "servant ministry", we know what we mean by that, but other people try to sort of distinguish that" (Respondent, *Area Group M*).

Within this shared spiritual community of the Order, deacons emphasised that they learnt about their ministry from each other inductively. Several deacons described their ministry as something that was "caught" from being around each other, rather than being "taught" to them more formally in training institutions. One respondent indicated that because of this, a helpful change had been "clustering people together" in particular initial training institutions, to facilitate this learning from each other and as a group:

> I was the only deacon in quite a while when I was at [my] college and actually [this ministry is] something you'd learn and develop as a group. I mean I was involved in an area group; you know, within a group together, you can hear other people's experiences and build it from there, rather than [it being] something you can learn in a classroom.
>
> **Respondent, *Area Group M***

This same theme arose when deacons discussed the type of learning opportunities that helped them to learn their ministry. Deacons repeatedly emphasised the importance of placements and other forms of contact with other deacons; e.g.:

> Although there is the need for the theological and the pastoral and biblical training, because that is part of our foundation, there is [also] a sense of "catching" what being a deacon is, the experience. So I think attachments or placements with deacons [are] so crucial.
>
> **Second respondent, *Area Group M***

As a result, deacons often valued informal opportunities to exchange experiences, and some deacons were observed to seek out actively opportunities to share resources. Some opportunities arose within the life of the Order, such as engaging in conversations or running workshops at Convocation, and starting discussions around the edges of Area Groups to share resources and ideas informally.

However, this close bond and shared implicit understanding within the Order sometimes exacerbated problems in helping others to understand deacons' ministry. Deacons often relied heavily on this inductive mode of communicating the nature of their ministry to everyone, whether inside or outside the Order. As a result, they often had difficulties in explaining deacons' ministries more explicitly to those outside the Order, particularly to people with limited practical experience of deacons' ministries. This was particularly problematic given the diversity of deacons' ministries that this book has already explored. In this context, an encounter with an individual deacon did not necessarily give people within particular churches or Circuits an overview of what deacons' ministries collectively held in common. Many of those in particular churches may not encounter different deacons; those in this position were then limited in their ability to form an overview. Those that had encountered a number of different deacons were often reported by deacons to be confused about the diversity in outward forms of deacons' ministries they had observed.

At the same time, many deacons were often frustrated with those in local Circuits who hadn't yet "caught" what being a deacon was, despite multiple attempts by deacons to explain it. Many also recognised that others were sometimes frustrated with the ways that deacons had tried to communicate the nature of a deacon's ministry to them. This frustration extended beyond local Circuits to some of the Connexional post-holders, training institution tutors and others who weren't deacons who were encountered throughout the research. These occasionally expressed considerable frustration with what they saw as deacons' vague or insufficient explanations of their work to those outside the Order. The limited articulations of deacons' ministries were seen as particularly problematic because of the diversity in deacons' ministries and the tensions in relationships between ministries already discussed earlier sections in this book.

7.3.4.   Flexible Adaptation and Learning as One Goes Along

Given the diverse range of expectations placed on deacons both historically and in the contemporary context, the Methodist Diaconal Order placed a high value on deacons being able to flexibly adapt to different contexts and learn on the job. A number of deacons spoke of their ministry as something that they had to learn to do as they went along, in response to the needs in a particular place. The Warden also spoke of this, describing deacons as a "workforce where their primary skill is learning what is needed in that particular context". In this sense, learning was at the heart of what deacons did; for example, one deacon described how her ministry was not just to others, but also a "ministry to myself of learning new things" (Respondent, *Area Group M*).

This culture within the Order encouraged deacons to be flexible generalists, as one deacon described well:

> Some of us occasionally do *do* specialist ministry, but on the whole, what the appointments are looking for are generalists . . . You know, you [might be] doing family and children's [work] now, but next time you might need to do a load of lay training . . . [The Church needs] people who are flexible and people who can actually [have] transferable skills. Where you are lacking [these skills], you go and find them. And I think that's something that as an Order . . . we offer: this broad skill base.
>
> **Respondent, *Area Group D***

A broad matching was undertaken within the stationing process in which deacons' background and skills were one factor in where they were ultimately placed; however, this was only one of a number of factors, and deacons were expected to adapt as necessary wherever they were placed. As discussed in earlier chapters, this created considerable flexibility within the Order to respond to a wide range of different requests by Circuits. For example, when reflecting on the different types of appointment that were represented in one area group, and the way that individual deacons had to change depending on the appointment, one deacon commented that:

> I think that the commonality between them all is that they are all different . . . The commonality is in the discipline of being in a religious order where you are sent. So to actually say there is a commonality within diaconal ministry is difficult because we will all move into different [types of] appointments potentially every time we move.
>
> *Area Group J*

In principle, this included taking any additional training needed to respond to that context after they arrived.

One deacon emphasised how this constant changing had prevented her developing expertise in particular areas over the longer term that might have been an asset in her ministry. She described how this had sometimes been a barrier for her in her ministry, giving two examples. The first example given was a situation where her lack of a youth work diploma had prevented her securing funding for an appointment around thirty years ago. She then went on to describe a more contemporary example:

> At my last appointment, if I'd have got a diploma in counselling, I'd got doors into all sorts of other areas that I could have done. But knowing that my appointment was only for five years, by the time I'd have got my diploma, it would have been time to move on. So there are times when the rest of society wants somebody who is a specialist and you don't always fit the criteria. So I think this is one of the difficulties, isn't it, because we don't work in the rest of the world, we are working for the Kingdom of God, and you get on and do things and learn on the job, whereas the rest of the world wants somebody who has got the qualifications, which can be in conflict sometimes.
>
> **Respondent,** *Area Group J*

This created an environment where the Order sometimes used any previously existing specialisms that people may have brought to their ministry as a deacon, but was somewhat ambivalent to allowing deacons to develop particular specialisms in case these reduced their subsequent flexibility to go wherever sent. As this deacon commented:

> If you take out [the religious order dimension] and the collective discipline of being sent . . . you would start to get specialisms: [deacons saying] that "I only do this type of appointment." But because we are sent, really we accept what we are given and learn new things; it's a change every time.
>
> **Respondent,** *Area Group J*

Indeed, some deacons described how a lack of specialist knowledge or skills in a particular area could be a potential virtue. In their view, this was because they could then demonstrate to others in congregations (who also may not be starting with specialist skills) how anyone could learn to do new things, by learning alongside them to develop new skills where these were required.

A few deacons went even further, feeling training was unnecessary because they felt that when they were weakest and knew least, God would be strongest. However, many other deacons considered such an approach to be problematic, and expressed views that they should show good stewardship of the gifts and talents that they had been given. For these, this meant doing all they could to develop their own particular gifts and vocations to deal with their responsibilities.

7.3.5.   Initial Training and Formation

As the analysis above shows, a particular learning culture focused on flexibility had developed in the Methodist Diaconal Order, in response to the historical needs and expectations of the wider Methodist Church. This had combined with many deacons finding it difficult to express their ministry fully in theoretical language, and a focus on new members of the Order "catching" what it was to be a deacon by soaking it up through being around other deacons. In some ways, this created a strong formational environment, in which experienced deacons actively supported newer members as they went through student and probationer stages. It also provided a strong communal contribution to deacons' formation, locating them within a clear "community of practice" to support this process.[5]

However, it also raised several significant issues in terms of the process of initial training and formation which should be provided to those accepted as candidates for ministry as a deacon. The first key issue concerned how (and indeed whether) deacons could be trained for a role that is so diverse and contextual. Because deacons' practice was seen to look so different depending upon the context and role in each particular place, it raised real questions about how curriculums should to be structured to appropriately prepare deacons for the challenges of this ministry. One deacon summed this difficulty up succinctly by rhetorically asking "how do you train someone to be flexible?"

If deacons were seen as just being flexible "Jacks" or "Jills" of all trades, without substantive theory underpinning their role, then this raised the question whether *any* training curriculum or programme could be sufficient for meeting this challenge. It was certainly noticeable within the data that many deacons felt inadequately equipped to take on the challenges of their ministry after first leaving their training institutions. For instance, one deacon recalled the concerns she had experienced after training, noting how "the Methodist Church is going to release me and I don't know this, this, this!" (Respondent, *Area Group U*).

That said, deacons' experiences of initial training varied considerably, including significant differences in terms of when they had completed the training and which training institution they had attended. One deacon who felt they had had a particularly inadequate initial training programme said:

> The college said "We can't prepare you for everything" and I felt when I left "It didn't prepare us for anything!" We can't prepare you for every situation, no, but it would have been nice if we'd been prepared for some of the standard situations—baptisms, funerals, weddings. Nothing. If I didn't have a good colleague when I first started doing it, showing me how to baptise the baby, it would have been a real problem.
>
> **Respondent, *Area Group M***

Former deaconesses who had trained at the Deaconess Institute at Ilkley recalled a different experience, including being trained in practical skills that extended even to being a midwife (something which did not feature in any contemporary training programmes):

> Our training at Ilkley more or less encompassed all of that. I mean we had the biblical side and so forth and practical side as well including how to deliver a baby!
>
> **Respondent,** *Area Group D*

After the closure of the Institute at Ilkley, deaconesses and deacons ultimately became trained alongside presbyters. Even the more recently trained deacons pointed to both the positive benefits and negative implications of this practice. Positively, by being trained together, there was a belief that presbyters now have a better understanding of deacons (and vice versa), and a better relationship with deacons themselves. Negatively, deacons suggested that their own training was essentially designed around the training offered to presbyters, occasionally with a few additional extras added on because they were deacons:

> It feels like sometimes the slant [in lectures] is initially presbyteral and then we say "oh and deacons . . . "
>
> **Respondent,** *Area Group X*

> You quite often get the phrase "Oh, this doesn't apply to deacons" thrown at you when you [are at university].
>
> **Respondent,** *Area Group R*

This left student deacons having to negotiate on an individual basis with their training institutions to try to make the programmes relevant to them, whilst wondering what a more tailored programme for deacons might look like:

> I think the positive side out of a negative situation . . . was you had to learn to negotiate your way through [training], being with presbyters and thinking "well, what is the important thing [for my ministry as a deacon]?" . . . We were sort of able to tweak it a bit, but we did do stuff that perhaps we didn't need to do ultimately. But I don't think any of it was wasted. But I don't know how you would ever get a course that would be totally diaconal.
>
> **Respondent,** *Area Group M*

The difficulties of doing this negotiation and applying programmes to their particular ministry were exacerbated when deacons were located in training institutions where they were the only deacon, or in very small groups. Deacons particularly valued opportunities to learn not just from other student deacons, but also from more experienced deacons:

> I mean the fact that [one training institution] has got now a deacon going in [to lead] your tutorials is brilliant. They are understanding that deacons are different and have a different emphasis. And I think that needs to happen more and more in the institutions, the training institutions.
>
> **Respondent,** *Area Group U.*

> Something that's starting to change (I know I think they are doing now) is clustering people together, because I was the only deacon in quite a while when I was at college, and [this ministry is] actually something you'd learn and develop [better] as a group . . . I learnt more [reflecting] in the area group and trying to listen to deacons, but I didn't have that opportunity at college, I was the only student deacon and had no one to reflect with. My last year I managed to get . . . [a deacon] on board who was my tutor and so my final year, I actually finally spoke to a deacon, which was quite helpful. All my practical placements were with presbyters . . .
>
> **Respondent,** *Area Group J*

Many student deacons spoke frequently about finding the training incredibly hard-going, particularly for those students who were less academically oriented. Deacons' differing learning styles were an important factor in this, with one deacon who felt particularly strongly about this saying that:

> Training for me, sending me to college for four years, doing academic stuff was pointless. I'd have learnt a lot more [in other ways] . . . I was at [a university] for four years. Basically if I had spent a year and kind of put all that four years into one and then they'd have sent me out but with a [deacon as a] mentor or something who I would reflect a lot more with.
>
> **Respondent,** *Area Group J*

However, others had found aspects of their initial training more useful, and felt there was a need for longer training, but with more of a focus on including content that was specifically relevant to deacons and diaconal ministry. A few training institutions had begun to offer at least a limited amount of curriculum content that was designed specifically for student deacons. However, tutors expressed reservations about much of the existing material available to support such teaching, and overall there was no clear shared picture of what such content might helpfully contain. Student deacons and deacons who had recently left training institutions were keen for any such content to be seen more as part of the core programme in their training institutions. Some gave accounts where, even when specific content was provided for student deacons, it was not always credited towards their qualification, and sometimes done as an added extra which student deacons did in their own time. The Methodist Diaconal Order had provided a student handbook, which was intended to be a supportive resource. However, some students saw this as adding to their burden of work in ways that were not credited by their training institutions. All of this exacerbated the stress felt by some deacons anyway when going through the programmes, as many found these programmes very challenging. The extent of the expectations and time commitments were felt by some current and recent student deacons to be immense, particularly given shorter programme lengths introduced recently. One student deacon memorably commented about the pressures of being on such programmes that "it almost broke me", with other student deacons present at the time recognising similar pressures.

There were also potential dilemmas around how this content was structured for those delivering such content in a context of formation for different ministries. These arose because the more that only deacons were trained in understanding a deacon's ministry, and only presbyters trained in a presbyter's ministry, the less mutual understanding could be developed between different forms of ministry at the initial training stage. Training delivered just to deacons wouldn't necessarily communicate an understanding of their ministry to others, and similarly for presbyteral ministry. A balance of some shared training and some training focused on the particular foci of these ministries was generally felt by deacons to be helpful where this existed. Overall, deacons expressed the importance of training that was more focused on their particular ministry, incorporating some practical and applied elements, alongside more traditional core basic theological and ministry curriculum content. Where particular issues were raised as being important to be included in programmes at training institutions, these issues have been reflected elsewhere in this book. A number of respondents, including some deacons and those from the wider Church, highlighted the importance of theological education as a means of enabling those involved in various forms of ministry to engage critically and reflectively with such issues, with initial training providing a foundation from which ongoing learning can then grow.

7.3.6. Deacons' Engagement with Continuing Learning Opportunities

Deacons recognised that in one sense, they had to constantly learn to adapt to new situations: "The one thing that deacons do need constantly it to do some form of learning and training. I don't think anyone needs to tell us we need to do it because it is self-evident" (Respondent, *Area Group J*).

However, beyond their initial training period, in practice, the undertaking of any continued structured learning to support their ministry was often left very much down to individual deacons to arrange. This was despite a commitment within the Order's "Rule of Life" to making time for "study" as part of the rhythm of deacons' lives.

Individual deacons often described encountering barriers such as funding and time constraints when trying to access learning opportunities. Whilst certain funding opportunities were theoretically available to support them in accessing courses, for example, these funds were dependent on deacons proactively applying for them. This involved deacons having to make a case for being awarded the funding, which was seen as a barrier. In such processes, deacons felt they had to justify why they wanted continuing training, not why they didn't undertake any. For example, one deacon commented:

> The Order doesn't really have the opportunity to do the kind of training [we need] . . . [As] a minster in active appointment, we get a grant every year, which we can use towards helping us to train in an area where we need it, but training is very much left to an

individual and that's one of my bug bears I'm afraid, because I think we need to be constantly updating and training.

Respondent, *Area Group H*

Deacons spoke of particular difficulties in being able to identify appropriate post-probation training opportunities and prioritise them. Within this, they often saw themselves as receiving little support or encouragement in doing so from those around them. The following exchange between two deacons in one area group provides one example:

> This is an area of tension for me because I'd love to do some form of training . . . I'm saying that . . . you know part of it is actually what kind of training. So it's knowing what's actually out there, then it's "okay how do I commit to that time?" if it's a weekly thing, for example.
>
> **Respondent,** *Area Group U*

> I find it very difficult to prioritise. For example, we've been offered a Chaplaincy Training Day . . . and I should have said "yes", but my week is so chockablock that week that I've said "no". And I find it very difficult to get the balance when there is an opportunity for training. It doesn't have top priority with me, I guess. If I really wanted to do it, I would make the effort and give it top priority, but I kind of feel when I look at my diary and think "oh no, those things are more important, I should be there". So I find it very difficult to know whether it's more important than I'm making it.
>
> **Second respondent,** *Area Group U*

Probationer studies was one area which bucked this trend, with a significant number of deacons citing their probationer studies as helping them to continue developing at an advanced level in a supported way early in their ministry. Some particularly motivated deacons had managed to negotiate ways forward to take on longer, more advanced courses after this. However, these deacons recognised that doing so depended on where they were, whether they could get the support of their Circuit, and the extent to which they were willing to take the initiative; for example:

Part of it depends on where your Circuits are ... [After] ten or twelve years in ministry, I needed something extra, and looked around specifically for something like that. When I found it, I rang the Super[intendent Minister] and said "I'm coming to you in September, I feel the need to do this given what you are asking me to do here ... but do you know there is a part time course on here that requires approximately one day a week plus block weeks once a term—would you be OK about that?" And he said fine. So in that sense, they gave me the time and the willingness. I paid for it out of my own pocket ... [with a contribution of] £450 from the training budget. I paid for [the rest of it] out of my own pocket, and I'm glad I did.

Respondent, *Area Group J*

There were also a small but significant number of deacons who shared findings from research they had conducted as part of higher education studies, and shared how this had influenced their own ministry. Sabbaticals provided another opportunity which deacons sometimes used to support learning and development.

Despite some good examples of sharing learning in places like Convocation, some other opportunities for cultivating collective learning exchanges between deacons were missed. For example, structures such as the Order's area groups offered potential spaces for building a learning culture integrally within the Order's life. However, in practice, such spaces were often recognised by deacons as becoming dominated by an over-riding emphasis on their role in facilitating mutual support. For example, one deacon commented:

The main function [of Area Groups] is support and fellowship. That is the main function of the group. Whenever there is a need for support, that is where they go and offload ... [learning] is not the highest priority. (Respondent, individual conversation)

There were also occasional tensions between the differing needs of active and supernumerary deacons in relation to these groups, which deacons generally worked hard to resolve.

At its best, the Methodist Diaconal Order acted as a significant practical resource for its members, with deacons able to communicate via meetings and the members-only section of their website to locate and share expertise. For example, requests observed on the website and informally in area groups frequently received swift responses. Those that posted these requests often acknowledged the subsequent responses as helpful. However, the practical orientation of many deacons sometimes manifested itself in ways which undervalued more formal learning. Internal discourses within the Order which specifically endorsed and valued more formal continued learning and training after the Probationer Studies period were noticeably limited. These limitations applied both in terms of the frequency with which formal continued learning and training was (not) mentioned, and the weight attributed to it in relation to other priorities when it was.

A minority of deacons occasionally expressed a reluctance to share perspectives on more conceptual or theological issues in public ways within the Methodist Diaconal Order if they thought that these might disagree with the views of more experienced, vocal or prominent members, and/or with the views of those in positions of leadership. It also became apparent that a very small number of deacons had become further disenfranchised as a result of conflict they had experienced from raising perspectives which they felt disagreed with the prevailing view. As a result, these few deacons had decided to avoid or disengage to some extent from aspects of the Order's collective life, noting that they didn't feel their views were valued or listened to. When this happened, it closed down otherwise useful exchanges that could have contributed to further learning in both directions. This was surprising, given that the Order was otherwise noticeable for the way it valued and integrated highly democratic and dialogical processes within its collective life.

7.3.7.   Supervision and Spiritual Direction

Another potential space for supporting growth in ministry was the deacons' commitment through the Order's "Rule of Life" to have a Spiritual Director. Many deacons found this a helpful discipline, even if they did not all consistently take it up. For example, one deacon made the following fairly typical comment:

> Spiritual direction too is quite helpful. I opt in and out of this
> depending on where I am really, but the times when I have had a

spiritual director, I've found that very helpful to encourage me to look realistically at what's going on . . . It is part of our discipline that we have a spiritual director, but it hasn't always worked out that way for me. But I have appreciated it at the times I have, and okay it was difficult to fit in a day now and again, but it was helpful and I benefited from it really.

Respondent, *Area Group U*

Others had found this less useful, and a number expressed some confusion over its precise purpose and the way it should work. The relationship between such processes and other forms of support and supervision was at times particularly unclear. As with ongoing training, deacons frequently stated that the onus was on them as individuals to set up and fund any spiritual direction or supervision that they received:

I think going back to finance, if you're having spiritual direction, you're having to pay for it. So there are lots of little things around— I'm not being mean—but you somehow end up having to pay for it.

Respondent, *Area Group K*

I have a group supervision with other professionals in other spheres, but I pay for it myself.

Respondent, *Area Group S*

Such forms of supervision and spiritual direction were necessarily not undertaken by anyone to whom deacons were accountable in a managerial sense. Indeed, deacons frequently described strongly resisting some models of professionalised line-management forms of supervision, whilst recognising that they had multiple accountabilities within their work.

KEY QUESTIONS

1. (a) What are the advantages of seeing ministry as being something that is more "caught" than "taught"? (b) What are the disadvantages of seeing ministry in this way? (c) In what alternative ways might formation, vocational development and learning in ministry be understood?

2. (a) What is the value of deacons becoming specialists in a particular field? (b) What drawbacks might exist as a result of developing any specialism? (c) What impact does specialization or generalisation have upon training?

3. What might an ideal initial formation programme for deacons look like, taking into account the deacons' perspectives in this book and wider understandings? What would it contain, and how might it best be structured and delivered?

4. How might the growing size of the Methodist Diaconal Order affect its ways of sharing together as a community, and how might it best adapt to this change?

5. (a) How might deacons best be supported to continue developing their learning in a wider range of ways, both formally and informally? (b) In particular, how might the Methodist Diaconal Order create opportunities to enable Deacons to learn from each other more? (c) How might the wider Church create more opportunities for those involved in different forms of ministry to learn from each other more?

7.4. CHAPTER 7 CONCLUSION

This final chapter has outlined some key elements within the formation, support, training and ongoing learning opportunities which form part of deacons' individual and collective experiences within the Methodist Diaconal Order and wider Methodist Church. Deacons shared how the process of becoming and growing as a deacon involved many challenges as well as joys. The flexibility required of deacons has encouraged deacons to value learning as they go along in their ministry. The collective life of the Order has created multiple opportunities for mutual support and informal sharing, as well as a common identity and space for nurturing deacons' spiritual life together. At the same time, it has created particular challenges for deacons' valuing of more in-depth learning, and for communicating their understandings to those outside the Order. It has also created challenges for the wider Church in identifying what key skills, processes and underlying understandings may need to form the foundation of initial teaching and preparation provided to those becoming deacons. More active promotion and enabling of learning as part of the Order's common life, including further developing and supporting existing and potential learning opportunities within the deacons' "Rule of Life", provide the potential to enable deacons to continue growing further. Within such opportunities, there needs to be a balance of opportunities which enable deacons to share with each other, and opportunities which enable deacons to share with those engaged in other ministries, lay and ordained, to enable the whole Church to grow in its diaconal ministry.

NOTES

1. For a copy of the "Rule of Life", please see Appendix D.
2. During the research period, deacons voted at Convocation to uphold the traditional understanding of direct stationing and itinerancy. At the same time, the Connexional Stationing Committee on the advice of the Diaconal Stationing Sub-Committee introduced a pilot scheme for one year that enabled deacons who were seeking a new appointment to indicate which of the available appointments they felt were more suitable than others. Further adjustments to this have since been made for subsequent stationing processes, in light of reflections on this pilot scheme.
3. This is the same deacon who was previously cited as feeling on the fringe of their local Circuit in Section 5.2.4, with this quotation indicating how the Order helped deacons respond to these feelings.
4. Supernumerary deacons are those deacons who have been given permission to "sit down" (i.e. stop being involved in full-time itinerant ministry, usually on the grounds of age or illness). A large number of these supernumerary

deacons nevertheless remained actively involved in some forms of ministry and in their area groups, to the extent that their age and health made that possible.

5.   For a discussion of "communities of practice", see Wenger 1998.

8.   CONCLUSION

Overall, this book has only been able to offer a summary of a deep and diverse range of perspectives on good practice from deacons in the Methodist Church in Britain. In the process, it has contributed towards an ongoing dialogue about ministries, the Church and the wider mission of God. Given the scope of these issues, it is perhaps not surprising that the research has raised as many questions as it has answered. However, the understandings that have been reflected here are shared in the hope that by reflecting on the way we speak about and understand deacons' ministries within this wider context, the Church might continue to learn how to reflect faithfully the Gospel in the current context. Indeed, the research process has sought to continually refine the questions being asked, so that these might provide an improved starting point for continuing dialogue. However, it is only through deacons and the wider Church reflecting constructively on questions such as these which enable this continued dialogue and learning to take place. Hence, this conclusion summarises the issues raised through the research, and highlights key implications for practice which have wider ecumenical significance as a basis for continuing and deepening this dialogue. Each group of implications is also related to specific recommendations that were made to the Methodist Church in Britain as a result of this research.

Deacons' narratives about their ministry showed rich understandings of incarnational ministry. Within their complex ministries, deacons saw the simplest acts as carrying the potential to convey their understanding of the Gospel in a powerful way. Through expressions of solidarity shown through presence and care through service, they described how they worked with others to discern ways for the Church to engage in mission and bear witness to this Gospel. Through relying on the grace and power of God in patient processes of unconditional and relational engagements with people, they described how they sought to reflect and respond to ripples of God's grace in these engagements. Moreover, an underlying purpose of making connections in a range of different senses emerged as a key purpose of their ministry. Through creating spaces and opportunities for connections to be made, they enabled new connections to be formed and existing relationships to be built between diverse communities inside, outside and on the fringes of churches. Through their particular concern for those who were marginalised, isolated, "on the edge" or disadvantaged in wider society, they enabled the Church to respond to the needs of these groups. However, equally importantly, they described how they sought to bring the concerns, perspectives and insights of these groups back to churches, and enabled mutual learning and growth as a result.

KEY IMPLICATIONS FOR PRACTICE[1]

These findings highlight the importance of those involved in the Church reflecting further on the relationships between these different aspects of the Church's mission. The development of deacons' practice can benefit from discussing these relationships with each other, and reflecting further together on their ministry in light of each other's diverse experiences and wider reading. In addition, opportunities for those involved in different ministries to engage in dialogue about their understandings are important for enabling them to learn from each other and work together more effectively. Further research into other roles within the Church, as well as the perspectives of those with whom the Church works, would add important additional voices to these discussions and the development of practice which can arise from them.

Deacons within this research saw their own identity, integrity and vocation as central to the process of good practice within their ministry. Many deacons reflected carefully on how they positioned and presented themselves to different individuals and groups, in order to reduce barriers to building relationships. This presented challenges where others saw this as blurring their identity. There were also risks that, in identifying with those who were marginalised, deacons themselves could end up "out on a limb" and feeling excluded, especially where the Church did not support them in retaining links. Historic experiences of deacons within the Methodist Church (which shared similarities with many other traditions) were seen as exacerbating this risk. A key related challenge for deacons was how to enable and encourage the diaconal ministry of the whole people of God, including lay people within the Church. Deacons in the Methodist Church saw their ministry as providing one focus for such work, having offered themselves to it in a full time, permanent way and been freed up by the Church to be available and flexible in modelling it. However, Church discourses of how ordained ministries represent the Church within wider communities sometimes risk not recognising or even excluding lay involvement. Deacons saw their ministry as being most effective when working co-operatively and collaboratively in teams with others, lay and ordained. This involved recognising different foci whilst negotiating over how these ministries connected together within a particular context. The more positive and inclusive approaches to understanding a deacon's role outlined in this report offer an alternative to approaches based on defining deacons in terms of what they are not, whilst retaining a clear sense of their particular contribution and focus, even amongst their considerable diversity.

KEY IMPLICATIONS FOR PRACTICE[2]

These findings reflect the importance of carefully designing deacons' appointments (including involving deacons in this process) to ensure that they are supportive of connections being made through this work, and don't isolate deacons from the wider support of the Church. Organising systems of training and support to help those involved in this process of designing deacons' appointments would be particularly helpful. Providing opportunities for those involved in diaconal work to be involved in the liturgical and worshipping life of the Church is also particularly important in maintaining these links once appointments begin.

More generally, the findings also indicate that is it important for churches to critically review their discourses surrounding representativeness in relation to ordained and lay ministry, in order to find additional ways of recognising and supporting the wider diaconal ministry of the whole people of God. Implications for improved team work include recognising both different foci and areas of overlap between different roles, and the need for ministry teams to negotiate with each other about how they join up their work. They also highlight the importance of clarifying Church discourses to support and encourage lay people in engaging in diaconal work, recognising that lay people are also involved in representing the Church alongside those who are ordained. In the Methodist Church in Britain in particular, this could helpfully involve both retaining the current full time stipendiary and itinerant role *and* finding further ways to recognise and support those who have leadership roles in diaconal ministry who are not necessarily doing this in full time stipendiary and itinerant ways. It is also important to recognise the impact that historical narratives and experiences have had on particular ministries, including deacons. This will support endeavours to better show the Gospel through the ways that those involved address historic issues and find improved ways of working together in the contemporary context.

Deacons gave accounts of their personal joy and often costly personal commitment to this ministry, which also affected those around them. The role of the Methodist Diaconal Order in enabling mutual support and providing shared discipline was crucial to them in sustaining and developing their ministry individually and collectively. Their common sense of belonging to the Order helped deacons to develop a culture in which formation was supported and reflection encouraged. The culture of flexible adaptation which developed in the Order helped deacons to respond to diverse and changing needs in local churches and Circuits. However, aspects of this culture sometimes inhibited deacons from engaging more deeply in learning, through not fully supporting deacons in practice to prioritise their engagement in more structured forms of learning over the longer term. In particular, the approach to continuing learning depended mainly on deacons identifying and applying for funds to cover their own training, which was often difficult and under-supported. Deacons expressed mixed experiences of initial training, whilst overall identifying significant limitations in the understanding and appropriateness of the training offered in relation to the particular focus of their ministry. Individual spiritual direction was another element of learning support that deacons were committed to in their "Rule of Life", but of which they had mixed experiences in practice. Some deacons accessed other forms of professional supervision or learning, and often found these helpful, but typically identified and paid for these themselves. Convocation provided some good opportunities to share in learning and worship, whilst recharging and reflecting collectively as an Order. However, limited other opportunities were identified which supported deacons in learning from others, and prompted deacons to share their collective learning with others outside the Order. Opportunities such as area groups within the life of the Order provided spaces for nurture, support and informal internal sharing. However, the mixed aims of these groups (including providing support and dealing with consultations/business from the Order) often displaced any focused or facilitated learning activity.

KEY IMPLICATIONS FOR PRACTICE[3]

These findings reflect the importance of churches actively considering what initial and continuing formational, learning, support and training opportunities might help deacons to continue to develop their ministry.

A key question to ask in addressing this is "How can we learn from each other more?", both between different deacons, and between deacons and others. In light of wider ecumenical debates about the role of a deacon, they emphasise the need for developing a clear curriculum which supports deacons in engaging with both their own ministry and its place within the wider Church and world. The findings also highlight the need to listen to barriers which may be limiting the likelihood of deacons engaging in such opportunities in practice. Overall, a positive and intentional approach to promoting different forms of learning between deacons, and encouraging sharing between deacons and others, is important in supporting deacons in developing diaconal ministry amongst themselves and others. The findings also emphasise the importance of structures for continuing mutual support in the challenges of ministry, and the need to continue to encourage and resource these.

It is such sharing and mutual learning between different perspectives that this research has sought to stimulate further. This has been done by encouraging deacons to share examples of good practice and challenges with each other, and by analysing and presenting the resulting accounts in ways that seek to improve the effectiveness of the way this learning is shared with others, including the wider Church. It is hoped that, in sharing these accounts, this important ministry can be better understood from the perspectives of those who have committed their lives to it, and hence often embodied its opportunities, tensions and dilemmas. In turn, it is hoped that learning from this experience may support all different ministries, lay and ordained, in working together, as they seek to respond to God's transformational and relational missional engagement with everyone, especially those who are marginalised in our churches and societies.

NOTES

1. The implications of the findings summarised in this paragraph were reflected to the Methodist Church in Britain in more detail in Recommendations 1–4 in Appendix E.

2. These implications were reflected to the Methodist Church in Britain in more detail in Recommendations 5–7 and 9 which can be found in Appendix E.

3. These implications were reflected to the Methodist Church in Britain in the more detailed and specific Recommendations 8 and 10 which can be found in Appendix E.

APPENDIX A. DEVELOPING COLLECTIVE LEARNING AND REFLECTION: A DIALOGICAL RESEARCH METHODOLOGY

This project sought to critically explore different ideas of "good practice" in diaconal ministry with deacons in the Methodist Church in Britain. The research approach that was used was developed from an innovative participatory methodology that had already been successfully deployed in earlier doctoral research by the lead researcher that critically explored understandings of good practice in Christian community work.[1] The concept of "good practice" warrants further explanation as to how it was used in this project. This concept fulfilled a range of purposes as a focus for this project, including:

1. providing a way in to exploring deacons' ministry within the research, as a form of inquiry into what deacons see themselves as doing and why.
2. providing a constructive means of provoking a critically comparative discussion amongst deacons about how their personal experiences and perspectives related to each other's.
3. drawing attention to the necessarily evaluative nature of any practice, in that every practitioner has to decide what they should do on a given day in their ministry or in a particular situation that they find themselves in. Practitioners necessarily do this in the context of their overall understanding of the ministry to which that they have committed themselves within the Church and wider society.
4. encouraging deacons to engage personally in critical and theological reflections on the accounts that they shared.

In this, the process sought to encourage deacons to bring together their diverse views and help to frame them into a collective narrative. By beginning to frame this narrative in a more explicit way, the narrative then becomes more available and open for continued exploration, clarification, challenge, improvement and comment.

A.1.   METHODS

The research was primarily undertaken through a range of group interviews with deacons, which were combined with participant observation at a wide range of relevant internal and ecumenical events.[2] The research process also included a literature review of wider writing about deacons in different denominations. This enabled the study to take into account a range of perspectives on the historical development of this ministry, alongside studies of different contemporary expressions of this ministry and accounts of related issues in different contexts, together with directly relevant theological and Biblical studies. These methods were supported by 18 initial interviews with key individuals and authors who were identified as being able to help set the context for the study.[3]

The area group interviews with Methodist deacons that formed a central part of this research strategy were conducted as part of the on-going programme of area group meetings that these deacons participate within as part of their "Rule of Life". Five initial observations of different area groups were conducted initially, followed by an additional 22 group interviews conducted using participative research techniques that covered all of the available area groups. These area groups involved a wide range of deacons, including student deacons, active probationer and ordained deacons, and supernumerary deacons. Each group interview began by asking each deacon present to share an example from their own ministry that they would consider to be "good practice" for a deacon. Within the subsequent discussions, particular attention was given to everyday issues and dilemmas arising within deacons' experience of practice. These were explored using critical reflective questioning to encourage deeper professional and practical theological reflection on an individual and corporate level.[4] The diversity of deacons' experiences and perspectives formed a central part of this process, as participants were encouraged to compare and contrast different perspectives as these were shared, and to consider how these perspectives might relate to each other.

Whilst focusing on the area groups as a main strategy for undertaking the research, the researchers were keen to ensure that everyone within the Order had an opportunity to contribute. Whilst every available area group was visited, there were a few deacons who could not contribute because they were not able to be present on the date of the researchers' visit. In addition, when carrying out the research, and particularly in the area group interviews, it became apparent that a very small number of deacons had largely disengaged from the collective life of the Order. So that their perspectives were not excluded from research which sought to engage with a diverse range of perspectives within the Order, the area group interviews were supplemented by two interviews conducted with deacons who tended not to engage with their respective area groups. These were identified through area group discussions and other research input, and their perspectives noted in context where raised.

All deacons were also given an opportunity to contribute individually in the early stages of the research through a short exercise during Convocation 2010. Information on the project was also circulated in the Methodist Diaconal Order's Order Paper, which is distributed to all deacons, with an invitation to contact the researcher if they wished to contribute further information or ask any questions. In addition, two opportunistic interviews were undertaken with deacons within their practice contexts. Engaging in these additional interviews and providing these other opportunities for input helped to check whether there were any significant alternative perspectives that may have received less attention because of the particular group-based approach taken.

At Convocation 2011, the emerging analysis of deacons' perspectives was reflected back to the Methodist Diaconal Order through a presentation and discussion groups. This enabled the researchers' emerging interpretation of the deacons' perspectives to be verified collectively with the deacons, in order to ensure that their views had been heard correctly and to explore further some of the issues and relationships within the data. Through these multiple opportunities, every deacon in the Methodist Diaconal Order had an opportunity to contribute their perspectives at least once.

All of the individual and group interviews were transcribed verbatim and systematically coded "line by line" using NVIVO qualitative data analysis software to highlight the common themes. Three different researchers (Andrew Orton, Todd Stockdale and Mark Powell) were involved in working with this anonymized data, initially analysing and coding sections of the data independently to enhance the validity of the coding framework developed. These analysis and coding structures were then brought together and confirmed to be compatible, highlighting common themes and forming a unified structure. These themes were then grouped into 8 overall clusters to help explore the connections (see Appendix B). The connections found between the themes then formed the basis for the structure of this report. This approach provided a systematic way of analysing the data which has complemented the emergent dialogical process undertaken, providing a way of developing and cross-checking the analysis in a verifiable way.

A.2.   METHODOLOGICAL REFLECTIONS: CONNECTING THE DIFFERENT VOICES OF THEOLOGY

Theological reflection was central to these rigorous methods. In undertaking the research process, the researchers have sought to work with the participants to bring theological voices into dialogue with each other. In particular, the research has drawn on the practical theological methodology proposed by Cameron et al[5] in bringing together "four voices of theology", namely:

- **Normative theology**—the Scriptures, the creeds, official Church teaching, liturgies.
- **Espoused theology**—the theology embedded within a group's articulation of its beliefs.
- **Operant theology**—the theology embedded within the actual practices of a group.
- **Formal theology**—the theology of academic theologians, in dialogue with other disciplines.

The questioning and dialogue generated by the research process encouraged deacons to consider how their understandings of their ministry related to those within Scripture and the wider Church, both historically and in the contemporary period. By using practical examples of good practice and participant observation methods, the research sought to engage with deacons' practice as it was enacted. By engaging with official Methodist Church and wider ecumenical documents, the research sought to engage with the normative voices relevant to this practice. By ensuring the questioning was informed by the wider literature review described earlier, and locating the resulting critical discussions within these broader debates, including those over the interpretation of related Scripture, the research sought to engage with the formal voices of theology. By listening carefully to the voices and narratives from the ministry of those who are deacons, the research has sought to faithfully represent these voices, whilst also setting them in a constructively critical context. This approach has been underpinned by the broad theoretical methodology to qualitative research in practical theology outlined by Swinton and Mowat.[6]

These different "voices" have been combined in an integrated way in the following report and in the related outputs, with a different emphasis and starting place in each. For example, one academic journal article arising from the project focuses more on critically comparing the formal and normative voices, using these as a starting point for considering the Methodist Diaconal Order's position in a wider ecumenical and global social context.[7]

In contrast, this book starts from the accounts given by the deacons about their own practice, building the analysis initially from these narrative perspectives.[8] The engagement with such perspectives is rooted in the recognition that there is a need for churches to engage more effectively and critically with the actual theological views and actions of those within and outside churches. These can be studied as they are expressed and enacted in a contemporary context, alongside the more formal and normative studies. In particular, the exploration of the interaction between these more formal and normative studies and the "ordinary theology" of not just those in wider society but also those engaged in ministry is crucially important.[9] Ministers' perspectives represent the operational understandings and lived expressions of faith that inform day-to-day decisions in all the messiness and challenges of ministry. These perspectives remain influential in practice whether or not the underlying theologies correspond identically with every exact facet of the particular denomination's doctrine of which they are a part. To encourage open sharing, deacons were offered confidentiality in that their contributions would not be personally identified with them. At the same time, they were made aware that whilst every effort would be made to anonymise identifying details, it could not be guaranteed that others would not be able to identify their contributions.

In communicating these voices within this book, it should be noted that deacons had considerably diverse ways of phrasing their perspectives, and some deacons clearly struggled at times to say clearly what they wished to express. This is hardly surprising, given that even the most articulate Christian struggles to comprehend (and is left without adequate words to describe) aspects of God. For example, Christians can struggle to articulate the fullness and depth of God's love, despite having deep concepts such as the incarnation through which this can be explored. Furthermore, within the group discussions, deacons often qualified or added to what the others had said, often in ways that the original speakers agreed with, whilst sometimes raising questions about what they had said or even disagreeing with their statements. Indeed, the research process sought to stimulate further discussion and improved understandings of each other's perspectives within the Methodist Diaconal Order, supporting deacons within the Order to find common voices in their diversity. Hence, the quotations of individual deacons and others cited within this book should be treated as precisely that—individual statements made within group discussions or other forms of dialogue in which deacons sought to express their own personal narratives, which were set within the broader context of data and perspectives from each other and all the other "voices" listed. Having said this, the comprehensive analytical process undertaken has meant that the researchers can be confident that the broad categories and overall analysis presented reflects major areas of debate and new insights from amongst those with whom we spoke. This is the case even if we and others would not necessarily agree with every voice that we quote, or the precise way that these voices sometimes put their views across. As such, we would not see this book as in any way the last word on the topic, but instead as a tentative contribution based on the listening we have done, to reflect back what we have heard and present it to deacons and the wider Church to think further in a constructively critical way about what has been said. It is our hope as researchers that reflection and discussion will continue and be helpfully stimulated by the process arising from this research, as a means of deepening our collective understanding of this important ministry.

A.3.   CONNECTING THE PERSPECTIVES OF DEACONS AND OTHERS: A CONTINUING PROCESS

As researchers, we were particularly aware that perspectives from those other than deacons were also crucially important to be taken into account if a more complete picture was to be built up. These other perspectives included those of others within the Methodist Church, including presbyters and lay people, as well as those with whom deacons work in wider society. Indeed, relationships between different forms of ministry, both lay and ordained, and the Church's interaction in wider society, in which deacons play a significant part, proved to be key themes of the research analysis. In order to retain a clear focus and manageable programme of work within the time available, the research focused primarily on exploring the deacons' own perspectives on their ministry. However, perspectives from the wider literature and individual interviews, as well as opportunities within the participant observations to observe significant interactions with others, all helped to set the deacons' own perspectives in a critical context. In particular, these wider perspectives helped inform the phrasing of constructively critical questions that were deployed by the researchers to enable deacons to reflect on their work in its wider context. In the process, the research sought to help to stimulate wider organisational learning by raising awareness of the issues facing those playing this particular role within it, including the dilemmas faced within this work.[10]

Throughout the research, the intention has been to encourage the findings to be considered and debated across the wider Church, so that they can be critically reflected on in ways that inform future practice. In order to explore how best to enable this reflection to happen, an initial briefing on the methodological approach was given to the Connexional Research Forum on 28 May 2010. This included a discussion on the ethics of the approach and how best to involve the wider church in the process. Subsequently, a presentation of emerging issues was made on 26 November 2010 to the new Ministries Committee that was being developed, to help this committee in its initial reflections on strategic ministry issues facing the Methodist Church. In the final stages of the project in September 2011, a major conference "Making Connections: Exploring Contemporary Diaconal Ministry" was organized at St Johns' College, Durham University. This open conference brought together 138 people to discuss different Methodist and ecumenical perspectives on diaconal ministry. The conference included leading national and international speakers on this subject, as well as inviting initial feedback from the wider Church on the project's findings.

Following the conference, a draft of the final report was compiled by the authors and then edited with the support of a reference group. The members of the reference group acted in their personal capacities (and not in any official capacity) as a sounding board in the process of producing the final version. To enhance the independence and rigour of the project, this reference group were offered access to scrutinize anonymized forms of the analysed data in ways that did not in any way compromise the undertakings of anonymity given to those who had participated. The role of the reference group was to help ensure that the report was phrased in a clear way to communicate well with different potential audiences, ask questions to help clarify the content, share their expertise and make recommendations that might improve the report's effectiveness. The final wording of the report (and responsibility for any errors) remains that of the authors.

The final report was presented and discussed at the Ministries Committee on 11 September 2012. It is hoped that this published version will further stimulate constructive debate on the perspectives and issues raised, and prompt wider research, reflection and action that draws in other perspectives to this debate.

A.4.　　FULL LIST OF INTERVIEWS AND OBSERVATIONS CONDUCTED

Initial individual interviews were conducted with:

- Methodist Diaconal Order Leadership Team members: Deacon Sue Culver, (28 October 2009), Deacon Margaret Cox (11 May 2010), Deacon Ian Murray (11 May 2010) and Deacon Karen McBride (04 June 2010).
- Deacon Kathryn Fitzsimons (Diaconal Association of the Church of England, Leeds; 19 February 2010).
- Deacon Jackie Fowler (deacon in the Methodist Diaconal Order and President, Diakonia Region Africa-Europe; 3 March 2010, London).

- The Revd Ken Howcroft (Assistant Secretary of Conference in the Methodist Church's Connexional Team; 4 March 2010, London).
- The Revd Howard Mellor (Discernment and Selection Co-ordinator in the Methodist Church's Connexional Team; 4 March 2010, London).
- The Revd Dr Pete Phillips (Secretary to the Faith and Order Committee of the Methodist Church; 12 March 2010).
- Canon Dr Paula Gooder (Biblical scholar; 22 March 2010, Birmingham).
- Deacon David Clark (deacon in the Methodist Diaconal Order and author; 23 March 2010, Bakewell).
- The Revd Canon Dr David Hewlett (Principal) and The Revd Helen Cameron (Co-director of the Centre for Ministerial Formation and Methodist tutor; Queens Foundation, Birmingham, 23 April 2010).
- Tony Tidey (Wellbeing Officer in the Methodist Church's Connexional Team; 28 Mary 2010, London)
- The Revd Dr Roger Walton (Principal, Wesley Study Centre; Durham, 29 June 2010).
- The Revd Dr Philip Luscombe (Principal, Wesley House; Cambridge, 8 July 2010).
- Doug Swanney (Cluster Manager for Discipleship and Ministries in the Methodist Church's Connexional Team; London, 8 July 2010)
- The Revd Dr Mark Wakelin (Secretary for Internal Relations in the Methodist Church's Connexional Team; London, 20 July 2010)

In addition, two interviews were conducted with deacons who tend not to engage with their respective area groups, and two initial visits were undertaken to deacons in practice contexts (19 July 2010 and 12 August 2010).

Initial observations of deacons' area groups were conducted with:

- Newcastle-upon-Tyne Area Group (23 February 2010).
- Darlington Area Group (26 February 2010).
- London Area Group (3 March 2010).
- Birmingham Area Group (17 March 2010).
- Manchester Area Group (23 March 2010).

Group interviews with deacons' area groups were conducted with:

Birmingham Area Group	28 September 2010
Bristol Area Group	2 February 2010
Darlington Area Group	13 June 2011
East Anglia Area Group	27 September 2010
Harpenden Area Group	1 October 2010
Lancashire and Cumbria Area Group	19 November 2010
Leeds and West Yorkshire Area Group	13 January 2010
Liverpool Area Group	23 September 2010
London Area Group	19 January 2011
Manchester and Stockport Area Group	7 March 2011
Newcastle-upon-Tyne Area Group	16 September 2011
Northamptonshire Area Group	11 November 2010
Nottingham and Derby Area Group	29 November 2010
Sheffield Area Group	22 September 2010
South East Area Group	13 September 2010
South West Area Group	15 March 2011
Southampton Area Group	30 September 2010
Stoke-on-Trent/Chester Area Group	12 April 2011
Wales Area Group	20 October 2010
Wolverhampton and Shrewsbury Area Group	6 October 2010
West Yorkshire Area Group	10 September 2010
York and Hull Area Group	14 September 2010

In addition, briefer conversations were had with deacons from Scotland and the Lincolnshire area during the course of the participant observation, as there were no area groups that were currently meeting in these areas at the time of the research.

Participant observation was conducted at a range of key events during the research period, including:

- Methodist Diaconal Order Convocation, 10 to 13 May 2010.
- Student Deacon Conference, 16 to 18 July 2010.
- Diaconal Candidates' and Probationers' Oversight Committee (27 April 2010) and Diaconal Stationing Sub-Committee (19 October 2010) process meetings.
- Chaplaincy consultation event which included deacons from the

Methodist Diaconal Order (5 October 2010).

- Training Institution Tutors' meeting, 7 to 8 September 2010 (including a group interview with these tutors).
- Selected Methodist Diaconal Order Leadership Team meetings (14 to 15 April 2010, 21 October 2010, 10 February 2011)
- Area Group Secretaries' consultation meeting (24 February 2011).
- Joint Implementation Commission ecumenical consultations, 22 to 23 April 2010.
- Other denominational/ecumenical gatherings of deacons, including:
  - the Annual General Meeting of the Diaconal Association of the Church of England, 2010;
  - the Roman Catholic National Assembly of Deacons, 24 to 26 June 2011;
  - the Diakonia Region Africa and Europe ecumenical gathering, 21 to 26 July 2011.

NOTES

1. For a critical review of the concept of "good practice", and ways of critically using this concept within related research, please see Orton 2008.
2. Please see the end of this appendix for a full list of all the interviews and observations conducted.
3. These individual interviews are also detailed at the end of this appendix.
4. The principal researcher, Dr Andrew Orton, conducted all of the individual and group interviews. Orton is Lecturer in Community and Youth Work at Durham University, with a background in professional practice, managing, teaching and leading consultancy work with a wide range of community organisations, including in Christian settings. This experience, together with the approach developed through his doctoral research, informed this process.
5. See Cameron et al. 2010, p. 54.
6. Swinton et al. 2006.
7. Orton 2012.
8. A full list of outputs from this project can be found in Appendix C.
9. Astley 2002.
10. This approach drew on learning organisation approaches developed by theorists such as Argyris et al. 1978; Senge 1990; Hawkins 1997.

APPENDIX B. SUMMARY OF CLUSTERS IN DATA ANALYSIS

- Cluster 1: Narratives of the past
- Cluster 2: Community belonging and bridging
- Cluster 3: Roles and practice
- Cluster 4: Identity positioning
- Cluster 5: Power relationships
- Cluster 6: Notions of change, hybridity, dynamism, fluidity and evolution
- Cluster 7: Individual motivations and circumstances
- Cluster 8: Training, formation and resources

Each cluster contained multiple nodes that represented the key themes found within that cluster, and which helped explore the relationships between them. These relationships led directly to the various sections of findings reported in each chapter.

APPENDIX C. OTHER CONTRIBUTIONS ARISING FROM THIS RESEARCH PROJECT

The research generated a range of other work in addition to this book. These are mentioned below to reflect the substantial wider constructive dialogue stimulated throughout the research process, which also contributed at various stages to the analysis within it:

- An article published in a leading academic journal: Orton, A. (2012) "The diverse and contested diaconate: Why understanding this ministry is crucial to the future of the Church", *International Journal of Practical Theology*, 16(2): 260–284.
- A conference titled: *"Making Connections: Exploring Contemporary Diaconal Ministry"*, held in Durham, 8 to 9 September 2011, which brought together 138 people to develop collective understandings further. Those attending included deacons, those involved in a range of other ministries, those in church leadership positions and leading speakers from a range of different denominations.
- This conference also led to the publication of a special edition of the online "Theology and Ministry" journal on the diaconate in 2013, incorporating various contributions to the conference. These included an article co-written by the authors of this book entitled "The Contemporary Nature of Diaconal Ministry in British Methodism: Purposes and Processes of Good Practice". This journal is freely available at http://www.dur.ac.uk/theologyandministry/volumes/2/
- A paper titled "Missional Engagement? The Practical Theology and Ethics of "Good Practice" for Deacons in the Methodist Church in Britain", delivered to the "Practical Theology" working group of the 2013 Oxford Institute of Methodist Theological Studies, held at Christ Church College, Oxford, and involving scholars and leaders from the Methodist Church around the world.
- Contributions to wider academic debate and development, including contributing to the research culture at the Wesley Study Centre,

participation in several national academic conferences, and delivering:

- A Durham University Doctor of Ministry Summer School session which used this research as a case study to discuss issues in undertaking practical theological research with doctoral researchers.
- An Oxford University practical theology seminar at Regents' Park College, Oxford, 7 December 2010.
- An open lecture as part of a St John's College series in Durham, 7 December 2010.
- Input into the teaching of the Diaconal Studies module in the Wesley Study Centre during the project period.

- A response to the Methodist Church's "Fruitful Field" consultation in December 2011 relating to the initial formation and continuing development of deacons.
- A presentation entitled "Challenging Research: Should it Affect Church Practice, and If So, How?" delivered to the conference "A Learning Church: Research and Church Life", organised by the Methodist Church on 14 June 2012.
- A paper entitled "Changing Practice? Reflecting on Participatory Qualitative Research in Diaconal Ministry", delivered to the "Qualitative Methods in the Sociology of Religion" session of the International Sociological Association conference, August 2012.

These illustrate the wide range of ways in which research such as this can contribute to theoretical and practical exchanges which help to further develop understanding and good practice.

APPENDIX D. THE RULE OF LIFE OF THE METHODIST DIACONAL ORDER[1]

As a widely dispersed community, deacons are united through their common Rule of Life. The Rule is not compulsory, but it is hoped that it will be freely followed and adapted to each deacon's lifestyle. It provides a framework for the hectic rhythm of everyday life and may become a blessing and a joy, bringing glory to God, Father, Son and Holy Spirit.

Devotional Life

We endeavour to:

- attend worship regularly, especially Holy Communion.
- set aside time each day to read the Bible devotionally and to pray, including a time of intercession for members of the Order.
- regularly set aside time for self-examination, a chance to look back and see where we have failed in loving God and our neighbours and to give thanks for blessings received.
- find a spiritual director/companion, who will accompany, help and affirm us, and make time each year for a Retreat or Quiet Day.

Discipline

We endeavour to:

- be sensitive to the needs of those close to us, our families, dependents and friends.
- be aware of and relate to, the community in which we live.
- acknowledge and enjoy God's gifts to us of time, talents, money and possessions and through God's grace be able stewards of these.
- order the rhythm of each day, month and year, to allow for study

and relaxation, weekly day off, regular holiday.
- attend Convocation (unless a dispensation is granted).
- participate in the life of area groups wherever possible and attend meetings.
- keep in contact with other members of the Order by giving or receiving of fellowship and support, by visits, letter or telephone.

NOTES

1. Methodist Diaconal Order *Rule of Life*, copyright © Trustees for Methodist Church Purposes, used with permission.

APPENDIX E. RECOMMENDATIONS TO THE METHODIST CHURCH IN BRITAIN

The following recommendations were included in the original report version of the text from this book when it was presented to the Ministries Committee of the Methodist Church in Britain in September 2012:

Recommendation 1

That the Church could theologically reflect further on the relationship between presence, service, discernment, witness, developing diverse forms of church and enabling others to become involved in God's mission. A key focus of such reflection could helpfully be the ways these different aspects can contribute to making a wide range of connections between the Gospel, the Church and wider society. There is particular potential for additional learning from reflecting on the ways that these elements are being combined in creative ways within the everyday lives and ministries of all the Church's members, as Chapter 3 began to highlight. This is especially true when combining these reflections more widely and systematically with the other "voices" of theology as described in Appendix A. One practical way of developing this could be for a group of deacons to work with others within the wider Church to produce some resources for the wider Church on these issues.

Recommendation 2

That deacons could reflect further, both individually and collectively, on the deacons' perspectives and the analysis of good practice presented in this report. Deacons should particularly consider the extent to which they agree with these, any ways that they think they could be developed further, aspects of them which they think should change, etc. and any insights which might be helpful to them in developing their own practice. The

Area Groups of the Methodist Diaconal Order provide a good potential environment in which these reflections could be shared and developed together.

Recommendation 3

That the Church could create/promote more spaces in which deacons, presbyters and those involved in lay ministries reflect *together* on their ministries. Within such spaces, it is important that these ministries consider how they relate and what they can learn from each other. This could include encouraging both Connexional and local/District-level opportunities where practical.

Recommendation 4

That the Methodist Church considers commissioning further research to explore good practice within a wider range of lay and ordained ministries. This would complement the empirical picture that has started to be developed here and support the collective reflections recommended. Additional complementary empirical research to explore the perspectives of presbyters and lay people on their ministries should be developed to set this research in a wider context, and enable the interactions between different perspectives to be further developed. There is also additional potential for further learning by engaging those with whom deacons work in the wider community within this dialogue about good practice in diaconal ministry. Listening carefully to all those with whom deacons work in a wide range of ways provides a key opportunity for building on the Church's learning, by seeking to ensure that all voices are heard and engaged with in dialogue, including those which can otherwise be marginalized.

Recommendation 5

That Circuit Leadership Teams work closely with deacons where they are appointed, so that appointments are well designed. In particular, the research suggests that well-designed appointments are those in which all those involved support each other in making effective connections across churches and wider communities. Within this, the wider Church should be particularly aware of the risks that deacons' ministry can leave them "out on a limb" if they are not supported to maintain these connections.[1] As a result, it is important that deacons are supported within the pressures of the ministry that the Church has asked them to do in a particular place. To further facilitate this, deacons and Circuits should proactively work together in designing prospective appointments for deacons, to enable them to be well designed in ways that reflect the principles of good practice considered in this book. Deacons from local area groups could offer to work more systematically with local Circuits who are considering appointments to support this. This could helpfully be supported by the provision of training for those deacons who do this work, together with some form of co-ordination between enquiries from Circuits who are designing prospective appointments and those available to respond to them.

Recommendation 6

That the Methodist Diaconal Order and the wider Methodist Church could work together to consider ways in which deacons and other forms of diaconal ministry might be appropriately recognised and included within liturgical practice, particularly considering potential learning from other denominations in this regard.[2]

Recommendation 7

That the Methodist Diaconal Order and the wider Church could helpfully critically review their discourses surrounding representativeness in relation to ordained and lay ministry, as well as additional ways of recognising and supporting the wider diaconal ministry of the whole people of God. In addition, the Methodist Church could consider whether it might be helpful to recognise some form of local diaconal leadership role, and how this might relate to existing understandings and structures.[3]

Recommendation 8

That the Methodist Church should further develop its programme of formation and continuing development for those involved in diaconal ministries (particularly deacons). This should particularly include a detailed consideration of what curriculum and approach to formation and initial training might best support the development of these particular ministries. This development should take account of the issues outlined in this research, wider theological debates and the demands of this ministry in practice, through focused dialogue between training institutions, deacons, relevant Connexional committees and others.[4]

Recommendation 9

That deacons and the wider Church should reflect on the impact that the Church's historic development has had on particular ministries including the diaconate, and endeavour to embed new narratives within their corporate lives which recognise the transformative potential of the Gospel within these.[5]

Recommendation 10

That the Methodist Diaconal Order could further develop opportunities for sharing and learning between members of the Order, alongside the mutual support offered. This could be done by reflecting further together on the question "how can we learn from each other more?", and making this a strategic priority to be maintained in the continuing development of the Order as it grows. Particular attention could helpfully be paid to facilitating learning from the diverse experiences and perspectives within the Order, encouraging deacons in engaging in continuing development opportunities, and seeking to encourage deacons to work proactively with others outside the Order to share learning.[6] Appointing a deacon or group of deacons to take on this particular remit within the Methodist Diaconal Order may be a helpful step in promoting this further.

NOTES

1. See Section 5.2.4.
2. For further information, also see the discussion in Section 5.2.4.
3. The key questions in Section 6.2 may be a helpful starting point for this reflection.
4. See Section 7.3.
5. See Sections 6.3.3 and 6.3.4.
6. See Section 7.3 in particular.

REFERENCES

Argyris, C. and Schön, D. A., *Organisational Learning: A Theory of Action Perspective* (Addison-Wesley, 1978).

Ascension Trust, "Street Pastors", retrieved 17 September 2013 from http://www.streetpastors.co.uk/.

Ascension Trust, "What Is a Street Pastor?", retrieved 17 September 2013 from http://www.streetpastors.co.uk/WhatisaStreetPastor/tabid/96/Default.aspx.

Astley, J., *Ordinary Theology: Looking, Listening and Learning in Theology* (Ashgate, 2002).

Avis, P., *A Ministry Shaped by Mission* (T & T Clark International, 2005).

Avis, P., "Wrestling with the Diaconate", *Ecclesiology* 5, 1 (2009) pp. 3–6.

Bäckström, A., Davie, G., et al. eds, *Welfare and Religion in 21st Century Europe: Volume 1. Configuring the Connections* (Ashgate, 2010).

Banks, S. and Orton, A., "'The Grit in the Oyster': Community Development Workers in a Modernizing Local Authority", *Community Development Journal*, 42, 1 (2007) pp. 97–113.

Barnett, J. M., *The Diaconate: A Full and Equal Order* (Seabury, 1981).

Bible Reading Fellowship, "Messy Church", retrieved 17 September 2013 from http://www.messychurch.org.uk.

Bosch, D. J., *Transforming Mission: Paradigm Shifts in Theology of Mission* (Orbis Books, 1991).

Brown, R., *Being a Deacon Today: Exploring a Distinctive Ministry in the Church and in the World* (Canterbury Press, 2005).

Burnham, A., "The Liturgical Ministry of a Deacon" in C. Hall ed., *The Deacon's Ministry* (Gracewing, 1992) pp. 67–87.

Cameron, H., Bhatti, D., et al., *Talking About God in Practice: Theological Action Research and Practical Theology* (SCM Press, 2010).

Charlton, S., "Diaconal Consultation: 21–23 April 2010 (Report to the Joint Implementation Commission)" retrieved 30 January 2012 from http://www.methodist.org.uk/downloads/ecu-2010-diaconal-consultation-160611.pdf.

Clark, D., *Breaking the Mould of Christendom* (Epworth, 2005).

Clark, D. ed., *The Diaconal Church: Beyond the Mould of Christendom* (Epworth, 2008).

Collins, J. N., *Deacons and the Church: Making Connections between Old and New* (Gracewing, 2002).

Collins, J. N. "Reinterpreting *Diakonia* in Germany", *Ecclesiology* 5 (2009) pp. 69–81.

Cray, G. (2013) "Fresh Expressions: An Introduction by Graham Cray", retrieved 17 September 2013 from http://www.freshexpressions.org.uk/about/introduction.

Croft, S. ed., *Mission-Shaped Questions: Defining Issues for Today's Church* (Church House Publishing, 2008).

Davie, G., *The Sociology of Religion* (Sage, 2007).

Diakonia World Federation Executive Committee, "Diaconal Reflections: How We Experience Our Diaconal Calling in Our Diversity" (1998), retrieved 8 June 2010 from http://www.diakonia-world.org/files/theologiepapier98english.pdf.

Diocese of Salisbury, *The Distinctive Diaconate: A Report to the Board of Ministry, the Diocese of Salisbury* (Sarum College Press, 2003).

Fitzgerald, K. K., "A Commentary on the Diaconate in the Contemporary Orthodox Church" in C. Hall ed., *The Deacon's Ministry* (Gracewing, 1992) pp. 147–158.

Francis, L. J. and Robbins, M., *The Long Diaconate: 1987–1994. Women Deacons and the Delayed Journey to Priesthood* (Gracewing, 1999).

Furbey, R., "Controversies of Public Faith" in A. Dinham, R. Furbey and V. Lowndes eds, *Faith in the Public Realm: Controversies, Policies and Practices* (Policy Press, 2009) pp. 21–40.

Gelder, C. V. ed., *The Missional Church in Context: Helping Congregations Develop Contextual Ministry* (Eerdmans, 2007).

General Synod Board of Education, *Youth a Part: Young People and the Church* (National Society/Church House Publishing, 1996).

Gooder, P. "*Diakonia* in the New Testament: A Dialogue with John N. Collins", *Ecclesiology* 3, 1 (2006) pp. 33–56.

Gooder, P., "Towards a Diaconal Church: Some Reflections on New Testament Material" in D. Clark ed., *The Diaconal Church: Beyond the Mould of Christendom* (Epworth, 2008) pp. 99–108.

Graham, E. D., *Saved to Serve: The Story of the Wesley Deaconess Order 1890–1978* (Methodist Publishing House, 2002).

Grierson, J., *The Deaconess* (CIO Publishing, 1981).

Guder, D. *Missional Church: A Vision for the Sending of the Church in North America* (Eerdmans, 1998).

Hall, C. ed., *The Deacon's Ministry* (Gracewing, 1992).

Hawkins, T. R., *The Learning Congregation* (Westminster John Knox Press, 1997).

Hiebert, P. G. "Sets and Structures: A Study of Church Patterns" in D. J. Hesselgrave ed., *New Horizons in World Mission: Evangelicals and the Christian Mission in the 1980s* (Baker Book House, 1979) pp. 217–227.

Latvus, K. , "Diaconal Ministry in the Light of the Reception and Re-Interpretation of Acts 6: Did John Calvin Create the Social-Caritative Ministry of Diaconia?", *Diaconia* 1, 1 (2010) pp. 82–102.

McRae, A. *De-Centred Ministry: A Diaconal View of Mission and Church*, DMin thesis, Melbourne College of Divinity (2009).

Methodist Church in Britain, *The Methodist Worship Book* (Methodist Publishing House, 1999).

Methodist Church in Britain, *Statements and Reports of the Methodist Church on Faith and Order: Volume Two, 1984–2000 Part One* (Methodist Publishing House, 2000)

Methodist Church in Britain, *What Is a Presbyter?* (2002), retrieved 9 September 2013 from http://www.methodist.org.uk/media/879672/dev-per-what-isa-presbyter-2002-15062012.pdf.

Methodist Church in Britain, *What Is a Deacon?* (2004), retrieved 9 September 2013 from http://www.methodist.org.uk/media/879666/dev-perwhat-is-a-deacon-2004-15062012.pdf

Methodist Diaconal Order, *The Methodist Diaconal Order* (Methodist Diaconal Order, 2010).

Morisy, A., *Journeying Out: A New Approach to Christian Mission* (Continuum, 2004).

Morisy, A., *Bothered and Bewildered: Enacting Hope in Troubled Times* (Continuum, 2009).

Nelstrop, L. and Percy, M. eds, *Evaluating Fresh Expressions: Explorations in Emerging Church* (Canterbury Press, 2008).

Newbigin, L., *The Open Secret: An Introduction to the Theology of Mission* (Eerdmans, 1995).

O'Toole, R., "The Diaconate within the Roman Catholic Church" in Hall, C. ed., *The Deacon's Ministry* (Gracewing, 1992) pp. 175–190.

Orton, A., *Faith, Dialogue and Difference in Christian Community Work: Learning "Good Practice"?*, PhD thesis, Durham University (2008).

Orton, A., "The Diverse and Contested Diaconate: Why Understanding This Ministry Is Crucial to the Future of the Church", *International Journal of Practical Theology*, 16, 2 (2012) pp. 260–284.

Renewed Diaconate Working Party of the House of Bishops, *For Such a Time as This: A Renewed Diaconate in the Church of England* (Church House Publishing, 2001).

Senge, P. M., *The Fifth Discipline: The Art and Practice of the Learning Organization* (Random House, 1990).

Staton, M. W., *The Development of Diaconal Ministry in the Methodist Church: A Historical and Theological Study*, PhD thesis, University of Leeds (2001).

Swinton, J. and Mowat, H., *Practical Theology and Qualitative Research* (SCM Press, 2006).

Wenger, E., *Communities of Practice* (Cambridge University Press, 1998).

Wittberg, P., *From Piety to Professionalism—and Back? Transformations of Organized Religious Virtuosity* (Lexington, 2006).

World Council of Churches, "Baptism, Eucharist and Ministry", *Faith and Order Paper*, 111 (1982), available at http://www.oikoumene.org/fileadmin/files/wcc-main/documents/p2/FO1982_111_en.pdf.

World Council of Churches, "Theological Perspectives on Diakonia in 21st Century", *Statement from the conference jointly organized by the Justice and Diakonia, Just and Inclusive Communities, and Mission and Evangelism programmes of the World Council of Churches, 2–6 June 2012* (2012), retrieved 6 September 2013 from http://www.oikoumene.org/en/resources/documents/wcc-programmes/unity-mission-evangelism-and-spirituality/just-and-inclusive-communities/theological-perspectives-on-diakonia-in-21st-century?set_language=en.